CHECKP○INT
MATHS
11–14

RIC PIMENTEL
TERRY WALL

Hodder Murray

A MEMBER OF THE HODDER HEADLINE GROUP

Acknowledgements

Every effort has been made to trace and acknowledge ownership of copyright. The publishers will be glad to make suitable arrangements with any copyright holder whom it has not been possible to contact.

Illustrations were drawn by Jeff Edwards and Josephine Blake

Photos
page i © Robert Landau/CORBIS
page 2 © akg-images
page 7 © George D. Lepp/CORBIS
page 20 © akg-images
page 34 © akg-images
page 82 © akg-images

The following questions are reproduced by permission of the University of Cambridge Local Examinations Syndicate: pages 182–3 question 3 and pages 183–4 questions 1–2. The University of Cambridge Local Examinations Syndicate bears no responsibility for the example answers to questions taken from its past question papers which are contained in this publication.

Orders: please contact Bookpoint Ltd, 130 Milton Park, Abingdon, Oxon OX14 4SB.
Telephone: (44) 01235 827720. Fax: (44) 01235 400454. Lines are open from 9.00–6.00, Monday to Saturday, with a 24-hour message answering service. You can also order through our website www.hoddereducation.co.uk.

British Library Cataloguing in Publication Data
A catalogue record for this title is available from the British Library

ISBN-10: 0 340 81293 1
ISBN-13: 978 0 340 81293 8

First published 2005
Impression number   10 9 8 7 6 5 4 3 2 1
Year   2008   2007   2006   2005

Copyright © 2005 Ric Pimentel and Terry Wall

Cover photo © Robert Landau/CORBIS
Typeset by Techset
Printed in Great Britain for Hodder Murray, a member of the Hodder Headline Group,
338 Euston Road, London NW1 3BH by Arrowsmith.

Papers used in this book are natural, renewable and recyclable products. They are made from wood grown in sustainable forests. The logging and manufacturing processes conform to the environmental regulations of the country of origin.

Introduction

This series of three textbooks has been written specifically for students in schools outside Great Britain. As with *IGCSE Mathematics* and *Core Mathematics*, we consulted teachers in many countries before we started to write the books. We wanted to know what they thought such a series should contain. We were given many suggestions on content, layout, reviews and the level of work; we have incorporated these suggestions into *Checkpoint Maths*. The major points on which most teachers agreed were:

- That the books should cover all the work outlined in the Curriculum Framework for Mathematics produced by University of Cambridge International Examinations (CIE) board.
- That this framework, the essential underlying structure to the course, should be extended where appropriate to help to motivate more able pupils. This extension material is flagged by a stripy line (on the right), if it appears in the main text or by an asterisk (on the left), if it is an isolated question in an exercise. It is also highlighted by asterisks in the summaries. Chapters containing some extension material are also marked with an asterisk on the Contents page. In addition, this third textbook has a special 'Extension' section (Section Six) which can be used throughout the year to stretch more able students or after the CHECKPOINT tests have been taken.
- That the work covered should be shown to have applications related to the subject matter. Investigations have been included at the end of each section.
- That Information and Communication Technology, ICT, should form an integrated part of the course and should not simply be 'bolted on' to the end of the book. ICT activities have been included at the end of each section.

Our intention is to produce a series of books that are rigorous, thorough and will interest and inform students of the value and place of mathematics in society.

Ric Pimentel and Terry Wall, 2005

Notes from the Principal Examiner

The CHECKPOINT tests are carefully written to help you and your teacher discover any areas where you need to ask for extra help. We do not try to 'catch you out' so please work with us to help you! The following points might help you:

- Always read the question carefully. Decide what we are trying to test and how best to find an answer. Then read the question again – you would be surprised how many of you actually make up your own questions instead of doing mine!
- Show your working – even if you use a calculator. We often give credit for correct working even if your final answer is wrong.
- Dont worry if you can't do a question – you may not have covered this topic yet so you can't be expected to know what to do!

- After you finish the test check through again to see that you have answered as many of the questions as you can. If there is time, check to see if your answers are 'reasonable' and then see if there are any more that you could have a go at.
- After the test is over, don't worry if your friends got different answers – you may be the only person to get it right! Remember, there is no pass or fail with CHECKPOINT we are just trying to help.
- When we have marked your papers we send some very detailed results back to your teacher so that you can get together and try to fill in any gaps in your knowledge.

I have spent my whole career teaching Mathematics and I love it – I hope that some of my enthusiasm will rub off on you!

Principal Examiner, 2005

Contents

SECTION FIVE – REVISION

* SECTION SIX – EXTENSION

SECTION SEVEN – CHECKPOINT QUESTIONS

SECTION ONE

Algebra 1

Positive indices and the zero index

Girolamo Cardano (1501–1576)

Girolamo Cardano was a famous Italian mathematician. In 1545 he published a book *Ars Magna* (Great Art) in which he showed calculations involving solutions to cubic equations (equations of the form $ax^3 + bx^2 + cx + d = 0$) and quartic equations ($ax^4 + bx^3 + cx^2 + dx + e = 0$).

His book is one of the key historical texts on algebra. It was the first algebraic text written in Latin.

Because of Cardano's interest in astrology, he was arrested for heresy in 1570 and no other work of his was ever published.

Al-Karkhi was one of the greatest Arab mathematicians. He lived in the eleventh century. He wrote many books on algebra and developed a theory of indices and a method of finding square roots.

In the expression $ax^4 + bx^3 + cx^2 + dx + e$, the small numbers 4, 3 and 2 are called **indices**. Indices is the plural of **index**. So

x^4 has index 4
x^3 has index 3
x^2 has index 2

Although x does not appear to have an index, in fact it has index 1 but this is not usually written, so

$x = x^1$ has index 1

The **index** is the power to which a number is raised. In 5^3 the number 5 is raised to the power of 3, which means $5 \times 5 \times 5$. The 3 is known as the index; the 5 is known as the **base**. Here are some examples.

$$5^3 = 5 \times 5 \times 5 = 125$$
$$7^4 = 7 \times 7 \times 7 \times 7 = 2401$$
$$3^1 = 3$$
$$a^5 = a \times a \times a \times a \times a$$

Laws of indices

When working with numbers or expressions involving indices there are three basic laws that can be applied. These are shown below.

- $4^2 \times 4^4 = 4 \times 4 \times 4 \times 4 \times 4 \times 4$
  $$= 4^6 \text{ (i.e. } 4^{2+4})$$

This can be written in a general form as:

$$a^m \times a^n = a^{m+n}$$

Note. The base numbers must be the same for this rule to be true.

- $3^6 \div 3^2 = \dfrac{3 \times 3 \times 3 \times 3 \times \cancel{3} \times \cancel{3}}{\cancel{3}_1 \times \cancel{3}_1}$
  $$= 3^4 \text{ (i.e. } 3^{6-2})$$

This can be written in a general form as:

$$a^m \div a^n = a^{m-n}$$

Note. The base numbers must be the same for this rule to be true.

- $(5^2)^3 = (5 \times 5) \times (5 \times 5) \times (5 \times 5)$
  $$= 5^6 \text{ (i.e. } 5^{2 \times 3})$$

This can be written in a general form as:

$$(a^m)^n = a^{mn}$$

Worked examples

(i) Simplify $4^3 \times 4^2$.

$$4^3 \times 4^2 = 4^{(3+2)}$$
$$= 4^5$$

(ii) Simplify $(4^2)^3$.

$$(4^2)^3 = 4^{(2 \times 3)}$$
$$= 4^6$$

(iii) Simplify $2 \times 2 \times 2 \times 5 \times 5$ using indices.

$2 \times 2 \times 2 \times 5 \times 5$
$= 2^3 \times 5^2$

EXERCISE 1.1

1   Using indices, simplify these.

(a) $4 \times 4 \times 4$ **(b)** $3 \times 3 \times 3 \times 3 \times 3$ **(c)** $7 \times 7 \times 7 \times 7 \times 7 \times 7$

(d) 6×6 **(e)** $12 \times 12 \times 12$

2   Write these in full.

(a) 7^4 **(b)** 3^3 **(c)** 9^4 **(d)** 6^5 **(e)** 11^2

EXERCISE 1.2

Simplify these using indices.

1 $2^3 \times 2^2$ **2** $3^4 \times 3^5$

3 $4^2 \times 4^3 \times 4^4$ **4** 5×5^2

5 $8^3 \times 8^2 \times 8$ **6** $6^3 \div 6^2$

7 $8^5 \div 8^2$ **8** $2^7 \div 2^6$

9 $10^5 \div 10^3$ **10** $3^9 \div 3$

EXERCISE 1.3

Simplify these.

1 $(4^3)^2$ **2** $(3^2)^3$

3 $(2^5)^2$ **4** $(4^3)^4$

5 $(3^7)^2$ **6** $(2^4)^4$

7 $(t^2)^2$ **8** $(m^3)^2$

9 $(p^2)^4$ **10** $(x^4)^4$

EXERCISE 1.4

Simplify these.

1 $2^3 \times 2^4$ **2** $3^5 \div 3^2$

3 $2^4 \times 2^2 \div 2^3$ **4** $3^8 \times 3^2 \div 3^4$

5 $5^2 \times 5^3 \div 5$ **6** $6^3 \times 6 \div 6^2$

7 $(3^4)^2 \div 3^3$ **8** $(t^5)^2 \div t^3$

9 $(m^2)^3 \div m^3$ **10** $(r^3)^4 \div r^5$

If the base numbers are not the same, only parts of the expression can be simplified. For example:

$$5 \times 5 \times 5 \times 5 \times 5 \times 3 \times 3 = 5^5 \times 3^2$$

$$p \times p \times p \times q \times q \times r \times r \times r \times r = p^3 \times q^2 \times r^4$$

$$m^2 \times m \times n \times n^4 \times n^3 = m^3 \times n^8$$

EXERCISE 1.5

Simplify these.

1 $3 \times 3 \times 2 \times 2$

2 $4 \times 4 \times 5 \times 5 \times 5$

3 $a \times a \times b \times b \times b$

4 $p \times 1 \times q \times r \times r$

5 $t \times t \times t \times t \times u \times u$

6 $7 \times 7 \times 4 \times 4 \times 4$

7 $a \times a \times b \times b \times c \times c$

8 $p \times r \times r \times s \times s \times s$

9 $u^2 \times uv$

10 $5^2 \times 5^3 \times t^2 \times t$

The zero index

The **zero index** means that a number has been raised to the power of 0. Any number raised to the power of 0 is equal to 1. For example:

$$4^0 = 1 \qquad 10^0 = 1 \qquad a^0 = 1$$

This can be explained by applying the laws of indices.

$$a^m \div a^n = a^{m-n}$$

Therefore

$$\frac{a^m}{a^m} = a^{m-m}$$
$$= a^0$$

However,

$$\frac{a^m}{a^m} = 1$$

Therefore

$$a^0 = 1$$

This can also be demonstrated using numbers:

$$5^3 = 5 \times 5 \times 5$$
$$5^2 = 5 \times 5$$
$$5^1 = 5$$
$$5^0 = 1$$

$\div 5$

$\div 5$

$\div 5$

Worked example

Using indices, find the value of each of these.

(a) $3^6 \div 3^4$ (b) $4^5 \div 4^3$ (c) $m^3 \div m^3$

(a) $3^6 \div 3^4 = 3^2 = 9$

(b) $4^5 \div 4^3 = 4^2 = 16$

(c) $m^3 \div m^3 = m^0 = 1$

EXERCISE 1.6

Using indices, find the value of each of these.

1    $5^3 \div 5^2$ 2 $3^8 \div 3^6$

3    $4^2 \times 4^3 \div 4^4$ 4 $2^4 \times 2^2 \div 2^6$

5    $3^3 \times 3^4 \div 3^7$ 6 $x^4 \div x^2$

7    $x^4 \div x^3$ 8 $x^4 \div x^4$

9    $p^2 \times p^5 \div p^6$ 10 $(p^2)^3 \div (p^3)^2$

EXERCISE 1.7

Simplify these.

1 (a) 4^2 (b) 11^2 (c) 3^3

2 (a) 3^4 (b) 10^6 (c) 5^3

Find the value of each of these.

3 (a) $5^2 \times 5^3$ (b) $3^5 \times 3^4$ (c) $6^2 \times 6^3 \times 6^4$

4 (a) $10^8 \div 10^3$ (b) $5^6 \div 5^4$ (c) $8^3 \div 8^3$

5 (a) $10^4 \times 10^3 \div 10^6$ (b) $3^8 \times 3 \div 3^7$ (c) $4^3 \times 4^5 \div 4^8$

6 (a) $(3^4 \times 3^5) \div (3^3 \times 3^4)$ (b) $(5^4 \times 5^3) \div (5^2 \times 5)$ (c) $(8^8 \times 8^7) \div (8^3 \times 8^5)$

7 (a) $(m^3 \times m^5) \div (m^2 \times m^4)$ (b) $(n^5 \times n^7 \times n) \div (n^6 \times n^2)$
   (c) $(p^2 \times p^3 \times p^8) \div (p^5 \times p^4)$

8 (a) $4 \times 4 \times 4 \times 5 \times 5$ (b) $7 \times 7 \times 8 \times 8 \times 2 \times 2 \times 2$
   (c) $5 \times 3 \times 5 \times 3 \times 5$

9 (a) $(a^3)^2 \div a^2$ (b) $(b^4)^2 \div (b^2)^4$ (c) $(c^2)^3 \times (c^3)^2 \div (c^5)^2$

10 (a) $u \times w \times u \times w \times u$ (b) $u^2 \times w^3 \times u^3 \times w$ (c) $uv^2 \times u^2v \times u^2v^2$

11 (a) $2^8 \div (4)^2$ (b) $2^4 \div 4^2$ (c) $9^2 \div 3^3$

12 (a) $2^2 \div 2^3$ (b) $3^4 \div 3^5$ (c) $2^5 \div 2^7$

2 Shape, space and measures 1

Measures of speed, distance and time; compound measures

We can measure the speed of a car in kilometres per hour (km/h). This is a **compound measure** as it involves more than one type of measure (in this case, distance and time).

A speed of 50 kilometres per hour (km/h) is a way of saying that the car will travel 50 km in 1 hour travelling at a constant speed. Other units of speed are miles per hour (used in Britain and the USA, among other countries), centimetres per second (cm/s) and metres per second (m/s).

We can represent the relationship between distance, speed and time on a diagram like this:

The layout of the diagram helps you to remember the formulae linking the three measures.

To calculate average speed, the formula is:

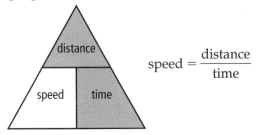

$$\text{speed} = \frac{\text{distance}}{\text{time}}$$

We can rearrange this to give the formula for distance travelled:

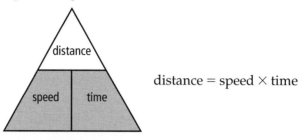

distance = speed × time

We can also rearrange the formula again to give time taken:

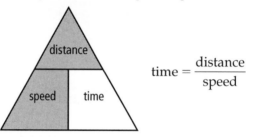

$$\text{time} = \frac{\text{distance}}{\text{speed}}$$

Worked examples

(i) Calculate the average speed of a car which makes a journey of 200 km in $2\frac{1}{2}$ hours.

$$\text{Speed} = \frac{\text{distance}}{\text{time}}$$

$$= \frac{200}{2.5}$$

$$= 80$$

The car's average speed is 80 km/h.

(ii) How far does a car, travelling at an average speed of 120 km/h, cover in $3\frac{1}{4}$ hours?

$$\text{Distance} = \text{speed} \times \text{time}$$

$$= 120 \times 3.25$$

$$= 390$$

The distance travelled by the car is 390 km.

(iii) How long does it take a train to make a journey of 720 km at a speed of 160 km/h?

$$\text{Time} = \frac{\text{distance}}{\text{speed}}$$

$$= \frac{720}{160}$$

$$= 4.5$$

The train's journey takes $4\frac{1}{2}$ hours.

EXERCISE 2.1

Do not use a calculator for this exercise.

Find the average speed of an object that travels:

1   80 km in 2 hours
2   300 km in 4 hours
3   650 km in 5 hours
4   70 m in 5 seconds
5   400 m in 25 seconds
6   150 m in 6 seconds
7   4 km in 30 minutes (give your answer in km/h)
8   12 km in 15 minutes (give your answer in km/h)
9   2 km in 1 minute (give your answer in km/h)
10   1.5 km in 30 seconds (give your answer in km/h)

EXERCISE 2.2

Do not use a calculator for this exercise.

How far does an object travel in:

1   2 hours at 75 km/h
2   $4\frac{1}{2}$ hours at 120 km/h
3   $6\frac{1}{4}$ hours at 80 km/h
4   30 minutes at 60 km/h
5   15 minutes at 320 km/h
6   1 minute at 120 km/h
7   10 seconds at 12 m/s
8   45 seconds at 60 m/s
9   2 minutes at 10 m/s
10   30 minutes at 20 m/s?

EXERCISE 2.3

Do not use a calculator for this exercise.

How long does an object take to travel:

1   20 km at 5 km/h
2   400 km at 80 km/h
3   15 km at 30 km/h (give your answer in minutes)
4   10 km at 40 km/h (give your answer in minutes)
5   50 km at 100 km/h (give your answer in minutes)
6   4 km at 40 km/h (give your answer in minutes)
7   20 m at 4 m/s
8   400 m at 80 m/s
9   10 m at 40 m/s
10   1 m at 40 m/s?

Density

Density is another compound measure. It is defined as the mass of a substance in one unit of its volume.

The formula for density is:

$$\text{density} = \frac{\text{mass}}{\text{volume}}$$

We can rearrange this to give:

$$\text{mass} = \text{volume} \times \text{density}$$

$$\text{volume} = \frac{\text{mass}}{\text{density}}$$

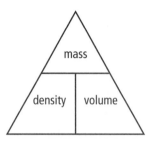

Units of density are grams per cubic centimetre (g/cm³) and tonnes per cubic metre (tonne/m³).

Worked examples

(i)   Find the density of a metal block of mass 140 g and volume 20 cm³.

$$\text{Density} = \frac{\text{mass}}{\text{volume}}$$

$$= \frac{140}{20}$$

$$= 7$$

The density is 7 g/cm³.

(ii)   Find the mass of a stone with a volume of 250 cm³ and density 5 g/cm³.

$$\text{Mass} = \text{volume} \times \text{density}$$

$$= 250 \times 5$$

$$= 1250$$

The mass is 1250 g.

(iii)   Find the volume of an object of mass 1500 g and density 7.5 g/cm³.

$$\text{Volume} = \frac{\text{mass}}{\text{density}}$$

$$= \frac{1500}{7.5}$$

$$= 200$$

The volume is 200 cm³.

EXERCISE 2.4

Do not use a calculator for this exercise.

Find the density of an object with each of the following masses and volumes.

1   mass 100 g   volume 20 cm^3

2   mass 400 g   volume 160 cm^3

3   mass 50 g   volume 2.5 cm^3

4   mass 8 tonnes   volume 2 m^3

5   mass 32 tonnes   volume 8 m^3

6   mass 27 g   volume 6 cm^3

7   mass 120 g   volume 15 cm^3

8   mass 30 g   volume 60 cm^3

9   mass 10 g   volume 1000 cm^3

10   mass 4 g   volume 2500 cm^3

EXERCISE 2.5

Do not use a calculator for this exercise.

Find the mass of an object with each of the following volumes and densities.

1   volume 20 cm^3 density 8 g/cm^3

2   volume 5 cm^3 density 4.5 g/cm^3

3   volume 400 cm^3 density 5 g/cm^3

4   volume 750 cm^3 density 8 g/cm^3

5   volume 0.5 cm^3 density 4 g/cm^3

6   volume 40 cm^3 density 0.25 g/cm^3

7   volume 30 m^3 density 4 tonnes/m^3

8   volume 8.5 m^3 density 0.5 tonne/m^3

9   volume 6000 cm^3 density 0.2 g/cm^3

10   volume 1 cm^3 density 1 g/cm^3

EXERCISE 2.6

Do not use a calculator for this exercise.

Find the volume of an object with each of the following masses and densities.

1   mass 140 g   density 5 g/cm^3

2   mass 280 g   density 7 g/cm^3

3   mass 350 g   density 3.5 g/cm^3

4   mass 200 g   density 25 g/cm^3

5 mass 50 g   density 25 g/cm^3

6 mass 1 kg   density 4 g/cm^3

7 mass 0.5 kg   density 5 g/cm^3

8 mass 8 tonnes   density 10 tonnes/m^3

9 mass 12 tonnes   density 24 tonnes/m^3

10 mass 1 g   density 1 g/cm^3

EXERCISE 2.7

1 A car travels 90 km in 2 hours. What is its average speed?

2 A train takes 3 hours 30 minutes to travel a distance of 280 km. What is its average speed?

3 A boy cycles at an average speed of 22 km/h. How long will it take him to travel 55 km?

4 How far will a girl walk in 4 hours 15 minutes at an average speed of 6 km/h?

5 An aeroplane flies over the Atlantic Ocean from west to east, covering a distance of 3800 km in a time of 6 hours 12 minutes. Because of the jet stream, it takes 7 hours 18 minutes to fly the same journey from east to west. Find the average speed of the aeroplane for each crossing.

6 A cube of side 5 cm has a mass of 1 kg. Find its density, in g/cm^3.

7 A ship of mass 20 000 tonnes has a density of 0.8 tonne/m^3. What is the volume of the ship, in m^3?

8 A man has a mass of 85 kg and a density of 1.1 g/cm^3. What is his volume, in m^3?

9 A piece of pig iron has volume 1500 cm^3 and density 7.2 g/cm^3. What is its mass, in kg?

10 A train travels for 2 hours 30 minutes at an average speed of 120 km/h and then for 5 hours 20 minutes at an average speed of 180 km/h. How far has it travelled altogether?

Shape, space and measures 2

Pythagoras' rule

Practical task

- In the centre of a piece of paper, draw a right-angled triangle.
- Off each of the sides of the triangle, construct a square, as shown in the diagram.
- Divide up one of the smaller squares as shown, making sure the dividing lines run parallel to the sides of the largest square.

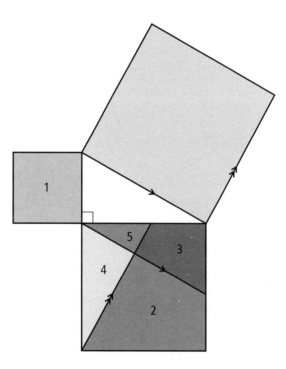

- Cut out the shapes numbered 1, 2, 3, 4 and 5, and try to arrange them on top of the largest square so that they fit without any gaps.
- What conclusions can you make about the areas of the three squares?

This dissection to prove Pythagoras' rule was constructed by Thabit ibn Quarra in Baghdad in AD 836.

Pythagoras' rule states the relationship between the lengths of the three sides of a right-angled triangle:

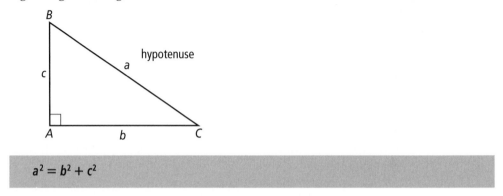

$$a^2 = b^2 + c^2$$

In words, the rule states that the square of the length of the hypotenuse is equal to the sum of the squares of the other two sides.

Worked examples

(i) Calculate the length of the side marked a in this diagram.

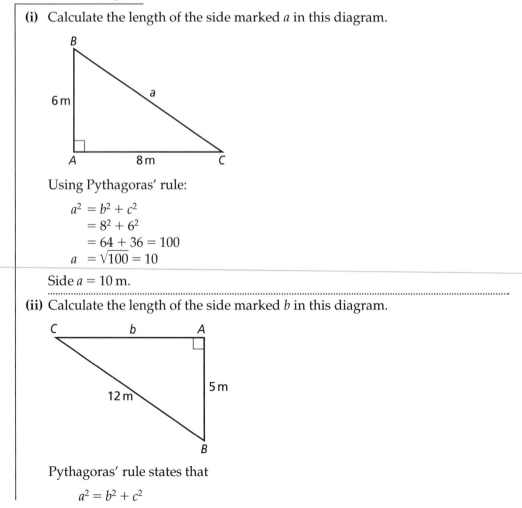

Using Pythagoras' rule:

$$\begin{aligned} a^2 &= b^2 + c^2 \\ &= 8^2 + 6^2 \\ &= 64 + 36 = 100 \\ a &= \sqrt{100} = 10 \end{aligned}$$

Side $a = 10$ m.

(ii) Calculate the length of the side marked b in this diagram.

Pythagoras' rule states that

$$a^2 = b^2 + c^2$$

Rearranging to make b^2 the subject gives:

$$b^2 = a^2 - c^2$$
$$= 12^2 - 5^2$$
$$= 144 - 25 = 119$$
$$b = \sqrt{119}$$

Side $b = 10.9$ m (1 dp).

EXERCISE 3.1

Use Pythagoras' rule to calculate the length of the hypotenuse in each of these right-angled triangles.

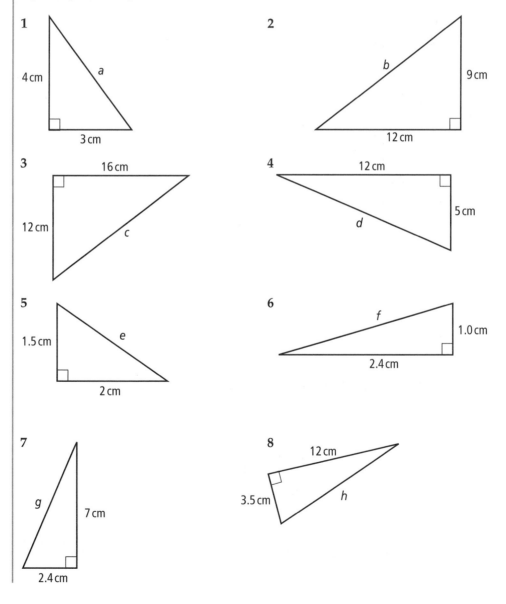

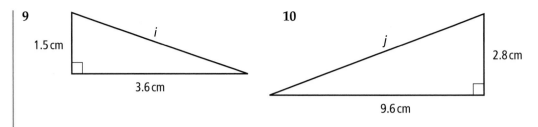

9   1.5 cm   *i*   3.6 cm

10   *j*   2.8 cm   9.6 cm

EXERCISE 3.2

Use Pythagoras' rule to calculate the length of the unknown side in each of these diagrams.

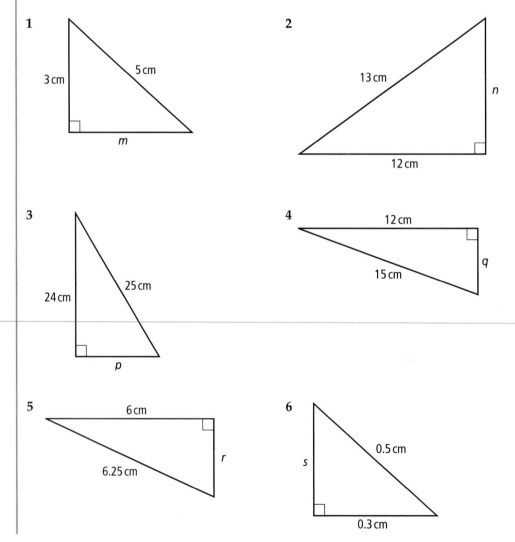

1   3 cm   5 cm   *m*

2   13 cm   *n*   12 cm

3   24 cm   25 cm   *p*

4   12 cm   *q*   15 cm

5   6 cm   *r*   6.25 cm

6   0.5 cm   *s*   0.3 cm

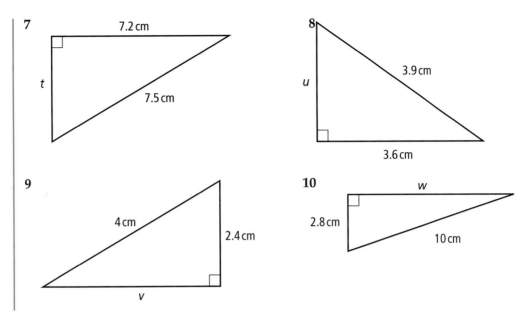

7 7.2 cm, 7.5 cm, *t*

8 3.9 cm, 3.6 cm, *u*

9 4 cm, 2.4 cm, *v*

10 *w*, 2.8 cm, 10 cm

Worked example

An isosceles triangle has a base of 6 cm and a height of 8 cm.
Calculate the length of its other two sides.

Draw a diagram to show the information.
Use Pythagoras' rule:

$$x^2 = 8^2 + 3^2 = 64 + 9 = 73$$
$$x = \sqrt{73}$$

The length of each of the other sides is 8.5 cm (1 dp).

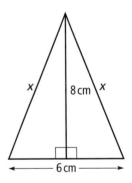

x   8 cm   *x*

6 cm

EXERCISE 3.3

For each of these questions, draw a diagram to show the information and use Pythagoras' rule to solve the problem.

1 A rectangle measures 8 cm by 6 cm. Calculate the length of one of its diagonals.

2 An isosceles triangle has a base of 10 cm and a height of 12 cm. Calculate the length of its other two sides.

3 An isosceles triangle has a base of 14 cm and sides of 50 cm. Calculate its height.

4 A ladder 7.5 m long rests against a vertical wall. The bottom of the ladder is 2.1 m from the wall on horizontal ground. Calculate how far the ladder reaches up the wall.

5   An explorer walks 120 km north from his camp and then 35 km east. What is the length of his shortest return journey to his camp?

6   A vertical mast is held in place by wires from the top of it to the ground. The mast is 60 m tall and the wires are fixed in the ground 25 m from the foot of the mast. How long is each of the wires?

7   The screen of a laptop computer measures 24 cm by 10 cm. What is the length from corner to corner?

8   A ship sails 360 km due south from a port and then 105 km due west. What is the shortest distance from the ship to the port?

9   A rectangular playing field measures 180 m by 37.5 m. How long is its diagonal?

10 A swimming pool is 20 m wide and has a diagonal length of 52 m. How far short is it of being a 50 m-long pool?

Worked example

In this diagram find the lengths of the sides marked p and q (in centimetres).

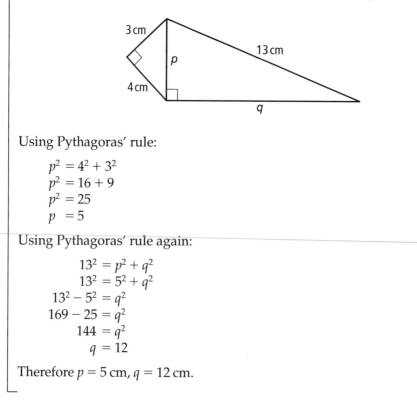

Using Pythagoras' rule:

$$p^2 = 4^2 + 3^2$$
$$p^2 = 16 + 9$$
$$p^2 = 25$$
$$p = 5$$

Using Pythagoras' rule again:

$$13^2 = p^2 + q^2$$
$$13^2 = 5^2 + q^2$$
$$13^2 - 5^2 = q^2$$
$$169 - 25 = q^2$$
$$144 = q^2$$
$$q = 12$$

Therefore $p = 5$ cm, $q = 12$ cm.

Find the lengths of the unknown sides in each of these diagrams.

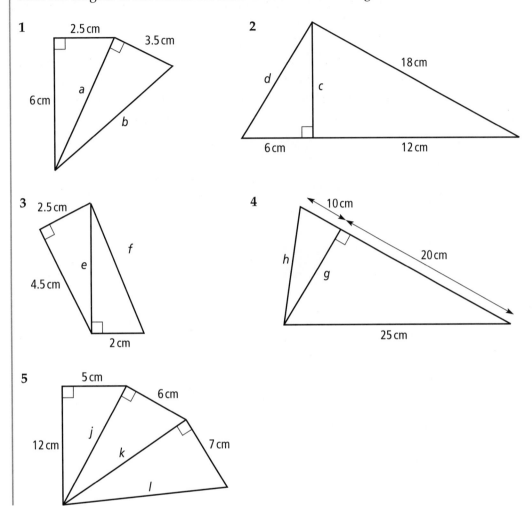

1 2.5 cm 3.5 cm 6 cm a b

2 d c 18 cm 6 cm 12 cm

3 2.5 cm e f 4.5 cm 2 cm

4 10 cm h g 20 cm 25 cm

5 5 cm 6 cm j 12 cm k 7 cm l

Shape, space and measures 3

Bearings and maps

In the days when travelling and exploration were carried out on the world's oceans, **compass bearings** (directions), like those shown in the diagram, were used:

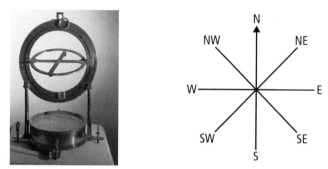

For greater accuracy, extra points were added midway between each of the existing eight points. Midway between north and north-east was north-north-east, midway between north-east and east was east-north-east, and so on. This gave the 16-point compass.

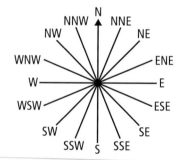

This was later extended to 32 points and even 64 points.

Today, however, this method of compass bearings has been replaced by a system of **three-figure bearings**. North is given a bearing of zero; 360° in a clockwise direction is one full rotation.

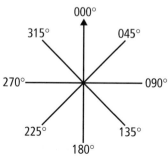

Measuring bearings

This diagram shows the positions of two boats, *A* and *B*.

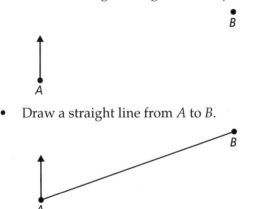

To measure the bearing from *A* to *B*, follow these steps.

- As the bearing is being measured *from A*, draw a north arrow at *A*:

- Draw a straight line from *A* to *B*.

- Using a protractor or angle measurer, measure the angle from the north line at *A* to the line *AB* in a *clockwise* direction.

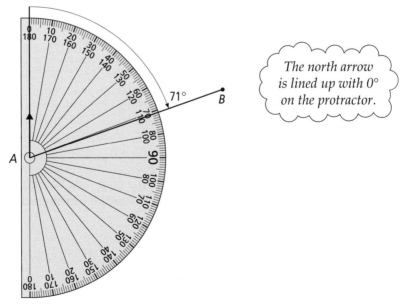

The north arrow is lined up with 0° on the protractor.

- The bearing is the angle written as a **3-digit number**. Therefore the bearing from *A* to *B* (or the bearing of *B* from *A*) is 071°.

EXERCISE 4.1

Copy each of the diagrams below. Use a protractor to measure each of the bearings asked for, on your copy of the diagram.

1 Bearing from A to B

               •B

  •
 A

2 Bearing from X to Y

           •
           Y

     •
     X

3 Bearing of Q from P

 •
P

     •
     Q

4 Bearing from M to N

          •
          M

 •
N

5 (a) Bearing from A to B
    (b) Bearing from C to B
    (c) Bearing from A to C

                    •
                    A

                               •
                               B

                •
                C

6 (a) Bearing from E to D
    (b) Bearing from E to F
    (c) Bearing from G to F
    (d) Bearing from F to D

                        •
           • E
           D
                       •
                       F

           •
           G

Worked example

This diagram shows two towns M and N on a map. The bearing from M to N is known to be 060°. Without measuring, work out the bearing from N to M.

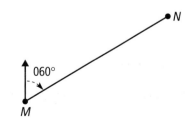

Extend the line *MN* and draw a north arrow at *N*. By using known angle relationships, you can calculate the bearing from *N* to *M*.

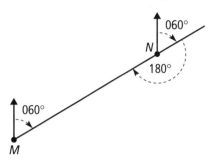

The bearing from *N* to *M* is 060° + 180° = 240°.

The bearing from *N* to *M* is known as the **back bearing**.

EXERCISE 4.2

1 Copy this diagram.

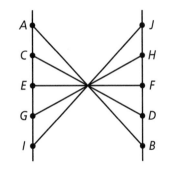

  (a) Measure the bearing from *A* to *B*.
  (b) Calculate the back bearing from *B* to *A*.
  (c) Measure the bearing from *C* to *D*.
  (d) Calculate the back bearing from *D* to *C*.
  (e) Copy and complete this table.

	Bearing		Back bearing
A to *B*		*B* to *A*	
C to *D*		*D* to *C*	
E to *F*		*F* to *E*	
G to *H*		*H* to *G*	
I to *J*		*J* to *I*	

  (f) Describe any patterns you can see that link a bearing and its back bearing.

2   For each of these bearings, calculate the back bearing.
   (a) 045°   (b) 090°   (c) 100°
   (d) 180°   (e) 105°   (f) 000°
   (g) 315°   (h) 213°   (i) 342°

3   This map shows a route through five villages labelled A, B, C, D and E.

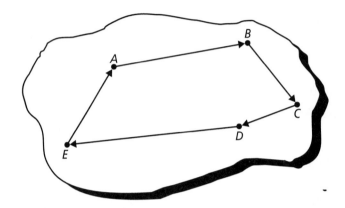

Some of the bearings needed to travel from one village to the next are given in the table below. Copy and complete the table.

Route	Bearing	Route	Back bearing
A to B	080°	B to A	
B to C	140°	C to B	
C to D		D to C	070°
D to E	264°	E to D	
E to A		A to E	212°

EXERCISE 4.3

For questions 1–3, draw diagrams using a scale of 1 cm : 1 km. Take north as a line vertically up the page.

1   (a) A boat starts at a point A. It travels a distance of 7 km on a bearing of 135° to point B. From B it travels 12 km on a bearing of 250° to point C. Draw a diagram to show these bearings and journeys.
     (b) If the boat wishes to make its way straight back from C to A, what distance would it travel and on what bearing?
     (c) Another boat wishes to travel directly from A to C. What is the distance and bearing of this journey?

2   (a) An athlete starts at a point P. He runs on a bearing of 225° for a distance of 6.5 km to point Q. From Q he runs on a bearing of 105° a further distance of 7.8 km to a point R. From R he runs towards a point S a

further distance of 8.5 km and on a bearing of 090°. Draw a diagram to
show these bearings and journeys.

(b) Calculate the distance and bearing the athlete has to run to get directly
from *S* back to *P*.

3 (a) Starting from a point *M*, a horse and rider set off on a bearing of 270°
and travel a distance of 11.2 km to a point *N*. From *N* they travel 5.8 km
on a bearing of 170° to point *O*. Draw a diagram to show these bearing
and journeys.

(b) What is the bearing and distance of *M* from *O*?

4 The map extract shows a part of Malaysia and Singapore. The scale of the
map is 1 : 4 000 000.

(a) A tourist travels from Kuala Lumpur to Singapore. By measuring the
map with a ruler, calculate the real (direct) distance between the two
cities. Give your answer in kilometres.

(b) What is the bearing from Kuala Lumpur to Singapore?

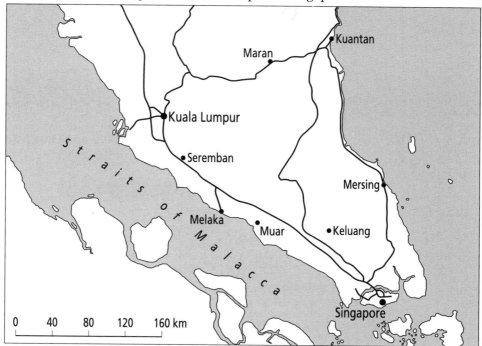

(c) The traveller decides to travel from Kuala Lumpur on to Singapore and
then Kuantan, before returning to Kuala Lumpur. Copy and complete
this table of distances and bearings.

Journey	Distance (km)	Bearing
Kuala Lumpur to Singapore		
Singapore to Kuantan		
Kuantan to Kuala Lumpur		

5   A light aeroplane flies from London to Cambridge and then on to Birmingham and Cardiff before returning to London again. The cities are shown on the 1 : 4 000 000 scale map of part of Britain.

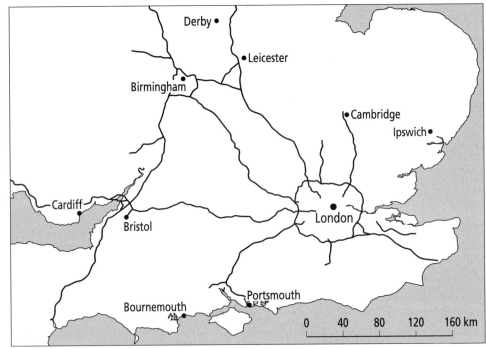

Copy and complete the table below by calculating the true distances between the cities and the bearings for each stage of the journey.

Journey	Distance (km)	Bearing
London to Cambridge		
Cambridge to Birmingham		
Birmingham to Cardiff		
Cardiff to London		

6   This 1 : 10 000 000-scale map extract shows part of southern Africa.

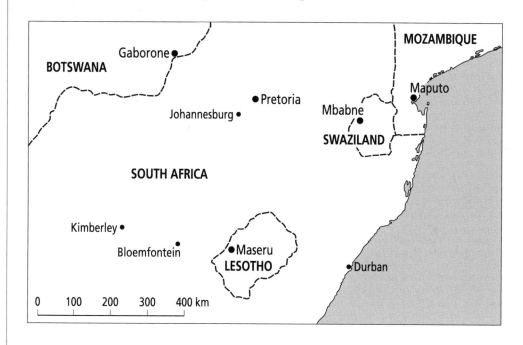

A businesswoman needs to visit the cities of Pretoria, Mbabne, Maputo, Maseru and Gaborone. The only conditions of the trip are that she start in Pretoria and end in Maseru.

Copy the table below and plan a possible route for the businesswoman by filling in the details of the route that she takes.

Journey	Distance (km)	Bearing
Pretoria to		
.... to		
.... to		
.... to		
.... to Maseru		

5

Using and applying mathematics/ICT 1

Investigation

The patterns below show a sequence of square patterns.

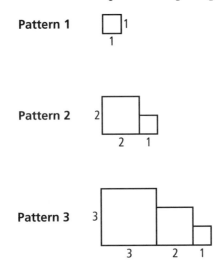

Pattern 1

Pattern 2

Pattern 3

1 Work out the total area of each of the three patterns.

2 Draw the next three patterns in the sequence and calculate their total areas.

3 Copy and complete this table for the first six terms of the sequence.

Position	1	2	3	4	5	6
Term (total area)						

4 Explain how the terms of your sequence are changing.

5 Predict the total area of the 10th pattern in this sequence.

* 6 Write the rule for the area of the nth pattern in the sequence.

ICT activity

You saw in Chapter 3 that Pythagoras' rule states that, for any right-angled triangle, the area of the square drawn on the hypotenuse is equal to the sum of the areas of the squares drawn on the other two sides.

For this activity use a geometry package, such as Cabri, to investigate whether Pythagoras' rule also works for areas of semicircles drawn on each of the sides of a right-angled triangle.

The picture below shows a right-angled triangle, with circles drawn on each side. The centre of each circle lies on the midpoint of a side. The diameter of each circle is equal to the length of the side on which it is constructed.

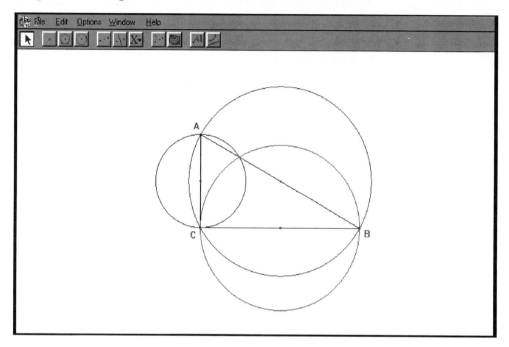

- Use the program to work out the area of each of the circles.
- Use these to work out the areas of semicircles drawn on each of the sides.
- Does Pythagoras' rule hold?
- Repeat the exercise with other right-angled triangles. Does Pythagoras' rule still work?

Summary

At the end of this section you should know:

- that the index of a number refers to the power to which it is raised
- the basic laws of indices:

$a^m \times a^n = a^{m+n}$

$a^m \div a^n = a^{m-n}$

$(a^m)^n = a^{mn}$

$a^0 = 1$ (also known as the zero index)

- how to apply the laws of indices when simplifying expressions
- the meaning of a compound measure
- the formula average speed $= \dfrac{\text{distance}}{\text{time}}$
- how to solve problems involving speed, distance and time
- how to solve problems involving density, mass and volume
- that Pythagoras' rule describes the relationship between the lengths of the sides of any right-angled triangle
- how to use Pythagoras' rule to solve problems involving right-angled triangles
- the three-figure bearing system
- how to measure and draw bearings
- the relationship between a bearing and its back bearing
- how to measure bearings and distances on maps drawn to scale.

Review 1A

1 Simplify these.
   (a) $3^3 \times 3^4$ (b) $5^7 \div 5^5$ (c) $(3^2)^3$

2 Simplify these.
   (a) $m \times m \times m \times r \times r$ (b) $p^8 \div p^5$ (c) $(x^2)^2$

3 Find the value of each of these.
   (a) $2^6 \div 2^4$ (b) $a^3 \div a^3$ (c) $10^4 \div 10^2$

4 Find the average speed of a car that travels 260 km in 4 hours.

5 How far does a train travel in $5\frac{1}{2}$ hours at 120 km/h?

6 Find the density of a block of mass 48 g and volume 5 cm³.

7 What is the density of an object of mass 75 g and volume 50 cm³?

8 Find the length of *AC* in the right-angled triangle *ABC*.

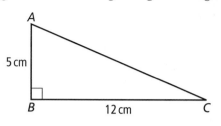

9 Find the length of *QR* in the right-angled triangle *PQR*.

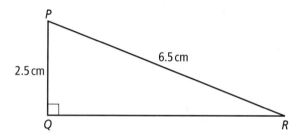

10 Ship *A* is 50 km from a radar station on a bearing of 345°. A second ship *B* is 20 km from the radar station on a bearing of 220°.

    (a) Make a scale drawing to show this information.

    (b) Find the distance and bearing of ship *A* from ship *B*.

Review 1B

1 Simplify these.
    (a) $2^4 \times 2^5$ **(b)** $6^5 \div 6^3$ **(c)** $(2^3)^2$

2 Simplify these.
    (a) $p \times p \times q \times q \times q$ **(b)** $m^5 \div m^2$ **(c)** $(t^5)^3$

3 Find the value of each of these.
    (a) $3^3 \div 3$ **(b)** $p^5 \div p^5$ **(c)** $5^5 \div 5^3$

4 Find the average speed of a train that travels 280 km in 4 hours.

5 How long does a train travelling at an average speed of 80 km/h take to travel 360 km?

6 Find the density of a piece of wood of mass 15 g and volume 20 cm³.

7 Find the mass of a stone of volume 60 cm³ and density 4.5 g/cm³.

8 Find the length QR in the right-angled triangle PQR and the length QS in the triangle QRS.

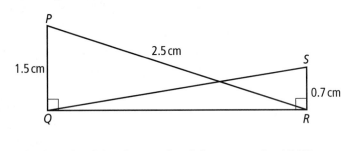

9 Find the length of the diagonals of the rectangle $ABCD$.

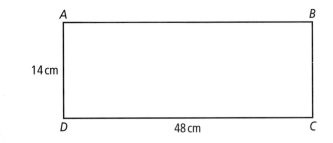

10 Ship A is 21 km from a lighthouse on a bearing of 065°. A second ship B is 13 km from the lighthouse on a bearing of 215°.
   (a) Make a scale drawing to show this information.
   (b) Find the distance and bearing of ship B from ship A.

SECTION TWO

Number 1

Standard index form

Galileo was an Italian astronomer and physicist. He
was the first person accredited with having used a
telescope to study the stars. In 1610 Galileo and a
German astronomer, Simon Marius, independently
discovered Jupiter's four largest moons: Io, Europa,
Ganymede and Callisto.

At that time it was believed that the Sun revolved
around the Earth. Galileo was one of the few people
who believed that the Earth revolved around the
Sun. As a result of this, the Church declared that he
was a heretic and imprisoned him. It took the Church
a further 350 years to accept officially that Galileo was
correct; he was pardoned only in 1992.

Galileo Galilei (1564–1642)

Some facts about Jupiter
Mass: 1 900 000 000 000 000 000 000 000 000 kg
Diameter: 142 800 000 m
Mean distance from the Sun: 778 000 000 km

This table shows the mean distance from the Sun of the nine planets in our solar
system.

Planet	Mean distance from Sun (km)
Mercury	58 000 000
Venus	108 000 000
Earth	149 000 000
Mars	228 000 000
Jupiter	778 000 000
Saturn	1 430 000 000
Uranus	2 870 000 000
Neptune	4 500 000 000
Pluto	5 910 000 000

As you can see from these examples, if numbers are written in the normal way,
the larger they become, the more difficult to read and more laborious to write
they are. They also become more difficult to compare in size. To overcome this,
we can use a method of writing numbers called **standard index form** (often

known as **standard form**). This involves writing numbers as a multiple of a power of 10, for example:

$100 = 1 \times 10^2$
$1000 = 1 \times 10^3$
$40\,000 = 4 \times 10\,000 = 4 \times 10^4$

It is important to realise that a number such as 40 000 can be written in different ways, all involving powers of 10, for example:

4×10^4 40×10^3 400×10^2 4000×10^1 etc.

However, only 4×10^4 is written correctly in standard index form. This is because, for a number to be in standard index form, it must take the form $A \times 10^n$, where n must be either a positive or a negative integer (a whole number) and A must lie in the range $1 \leqslant A < 10$ (i.e. from 1 up to but not including 10).

Worked examples

(i)   Write 580 000 in standard form.

Move the decimal point to the left until there is only one digit on the left of it (5). Count the number of moves (5). This gives you the index of 10 to use.

5.8×10^5

(ii)   Write 67 300 000 in standard form.

6.73×10^7

(iii) Write 1.8×10^4 as an ordinary number.

Move the decimal point four places to the right. After the 8 you will have to add zeros to fill the places.

18 000

(iv)   Put a ring around the numbers below which are written in standard form.

5.6×10^2 11.382×10^6 0.35×10^7 1.36×10^7

Only the two numbers circled show *a number between 1 and 10*, multiplied by a power of 10.

(v)   Multiply 300 by 5000 and write your answer in standard form.

$300 \times 5000 = 1\,500\,000 = 1.5 \times 10^6$

EXERCISE 6.1

Write each of these numbers in standard form.

1	65 000	2	72 000 000	3	84 000 000 000
4	700 000	5	4 900 000	6	812 000
7	24×10^5	8	0.67×10^8	9	40×10^5
10	0.07×10^5				

EXERCISE 6.2

Work out each of these multiplications and give your answer in standard form.

1   600×300

2   4000×2000

3   $500 \times 40\,000$

4   $7000 \times 6\,000\,000$

5   $2000 \times 25\,000$

6   $75\,000 \times 200$

7   $25\,000 \times 4000$

8   $3000 \times 400 \times 5\,000\,000$

9   $800 \times 6000 \times 200$

10 $(4000)^2$

EXERCISE 6.3

Write these standard-form numbers as ordinary numbers.

1   6.2×10^3

2   5.1×10^4

3   8×10^6

4   7.1×10^5

5   3.91×10^4

6   8×10^9

7   1×10^5

8   4.5×10^3

9   3.8×10^6

10 9×10^9

Using a calculator

You can use a calculator when you want to work with numbers in standard form. You can enter numbers in standard form and often, with large numbers, the calculator will present the answer in standard form too. It is important to know how your calculator operates.

Different calculators have different keys for standard form, but the two most common are $\boxed{Exp}$ and $\boxed{EE}$.

Worked examples

(i) Multiply 2×10^5 by 4×10^3.

$\boxed{2}\ \boxed{Exp}\ \boxed{5}\ \boxed{\times}\ \boxed{4}\ \boxed{Exp}\ \boxed{3}\ \boxed{=}\ \boxed{800\ 000\ 000}$

In standard form this is written as 8×10^8.

(ii) Multiply 6×10^8 by 4×10^7.

$\boxed{6}\ \boxed{Exp}\ \boxed{8}\ \boxed{\times}\ \boxed{4}\ \boxed{Exp}\ \boxed{7}\ \boxed{=}\ \boxed{2.4\ ^{16}}$ or $\boxed{2.4 \times 10^{16}}$

Note how your calculator displays an answer written in standard form.

EXERCISE 6.4

Use a calculator.
Write your answer to each of these multiplications in standard form.

1 $(2.3 \times 10^3) \times (2 \times 10^4)$
2 $(3 \times 10^5) \times (4.6 \times 10^3)$
3 $(5.8 \times 10^3) \times (5 \times 10^4)$
4 $(3.7 \times 10^4) \times (2.8 \times 10^5)$
5 $(4.1 \times 10^2) \times (3.8 \times 10^6)$
6 $(2.8 \times 10^2) \times (3.1 \times 10^5)$
7 $(2.7 \times 10^4) \times (1.9 \times 10^6)$
8 $(4.8 \times 10^3) \times (4 \times 10^3) \times (3.6 \times 10^4)$
9 $(4.8 \times 10^3)^2$
10 $(2.1 \times 10^4)^3$

The negative index

The study of astronomy presented a problem for scientists because they had to work with very large numbers. The study of microbiology and particle physics has given scientists a similar problem, working with very small numbers.

Fortunately, standard form can also be used to write very small numbers in a more convenient form, which makes it easier to compare sizes of numbers. Following a logical pattern, and using what we know about the zero index, we have:

1000	$= 1 \times 10^3$
100	$= 1 \times 10^2$
10	$= 1 \times 10^1$
1	$= 1 \times 10^0$
0.1	$= 1 \times 10^{-1}$
0.01	$= 1 \times 10^{-2}$
0.001	$= 1 \times 10^{-3}$
0.0001	$= 1 \times 10^{-4}$

*Numbers between 0 and 1 have a **negative index** when written in standard form. The **smaller** the number, the **higher** the negative index.*

Worked examples

(i) Write 0.000 37 in standard form.

Move the decimal point to the right until there is only one digit to the left of it (3). Count the number of moves (4) and make this a negative number. This gives the index of 10 to use (−4).

3.7×10^{-4}

(ii) Write 4.3×10^{-5} as an ordinary number.

Move the decimal point five places to the left. You will have to insert zeros to fill the places.

0.000 043

EXERCISE 6.5

Write each of these in standard form.

1	0.000 42	**2**	0.0004	**3**	0.000 087
4	0.005 32	**5**	0.000 000 8	**6**	0.000 76
7	0.000 008	**8**	0.000 000 77	**9**	0.0001
10	0.000 000 53				

EXERCISE 6.6

Copy and complete the following, putting in the correct index to replace n.

1 $0.000\,26 = 2.6 \times 10^n$ **2** $0.000\,068 = 6.8 \times 10^n$

3 $0.000\,000\,4 = 4.0 \times 10^n$ **4** $0.000\,493 = 4.93 \times 10^n$

5 $0.000\,000\,07 = 7.0 \times 10^n$ **6** $0.000\,006\,41 = 6.41 \times 10^n$

7 $0.004 = 4.0 \times 10^n$ **8** $0.54 = 5.4 \times 10^n$

9 $0.000\,000\,44 = 4.4 \times 10^n$ **10** $0.000\,36 = 3.6 \times 10^n$

Worked example

Change these to standard form and put them in order, *largest* first.

     0.000 46   0.000 083   0.003   0.000 742

In standard form the numbers are:

     4.6×10^{-4} 8.3×10^{-5} 3.0×10^{-3} 7.42×10^{-4}

Remember that, the higher the negative index, the smaller the number.

So, in order of size, largest first, the numbers are:

     3.0×10^{-3} 7.42×10^{-4} 4.6×10^{-4} 8.3×10^{-5}

EXERCISE 6.7

Put the ten numbers in Exercise 6.6 in order of size, with the largest first.

Algebra 2

Simultaneous equations

Solving simultaneous equations by elimination

Here are three examples of linear equations.

$$p + 7 = 11 \qquad 2(m + 3) = 4(4 - 2m) \qquad \frac{2(r - 5)}{2} = 2$$

Each of these equations has only one unknown, p, m or r, and can be solved by applying simple rules. In each case there is only one solution ($p = 4$, $m = 1$, $r = 7$).

The equation below has two unknowns (sometimes called **variables**).

$$2a + 3b = 22$$

It has a number of possible solutions, for example:

$a = 2, b = 6$	**or**	$a = 5, b = 4$
$2a + 3b = 22$		$2a + 3b = 22$
$(2 \times 2) + (3 \times 6)$		$(2 \times 5) + (3 \times 4)$
$= 4 + 18 = 22$ ✓		$= 10 + 12 = 22$ ✓

We know these solutions are correct because, in each case, when the values are substituted, the left-hand side of the equation equals the right-hand side.

However, if there are *two* equations, *both* involving the same two unknowns, they are called **simultaneous equations**.

$$2a + 3b = 22 \qquad \text{equation 1}$$
$$2a + b = 14 \qquad \text{equation 2}$$

How can we find a solution which satisfies both equations?

Try $a = 2$, $b = 6$ in equation 1:
$$2a + 3b = 22$$
$$(2 \times 2) + (3 \times 6)$$
$$= 4 + 18 = 22 \; ✓$$

Try $a = 2$, $b = 6$ in equation 2:
$$2a + b = 14$$
$$(2 \times 2) + 6$$
$$= 4 + 6 = 10$$
$$10 \neq 14 \; ✗$$

The value of the left-hand side does not equal the right-hand side, so that solution does not work.

Try $a = 5$, $b = 4$ in the two equations. What do you find?

In this case, there is only one solution that satisfies both equations simultaneously. The method of trying lots of different possible solutions is called **trial and improvement**. It works but it takes a long time.

A better method is called the method of **elimination**.

Look at these two simultaneous equations.

$$3p + q = 17 \qquad \text{equation 1}$$
$$5p - q = 15 \qquad \text{equation 2}$$

If you add the two equations, you will find that one of the variables (q) is **eliminated**:

$$
\begin{array}{rl}
& 3p + q = 17 \\
+ & 5p - q = 15 \\
\hline
& 8p \quad\;\; = 32
\end{array}
$$

Therefore $p = 4$.

To find the value of q, substitute $p = 4$ into equation 1:

$$
\begin{aligned}
3p + q &= 17 \\
(3 \times 4) + q &= 17 \\
q &= 17 - 12 \\
&= 5
\end{aligned}
$$

So $p = 4$ and $q = 5$.

Check in equation 2 by substituting $p = 4$, $q = 5$:

$$
\begin{aligned}
5p - q &= 15 \\
20 - 5 &= 15 \; \checkmark
\end{aligned}
$$

EXERCISE 7.1

Solve each of these pairs of simultaneous equations by elimination.

1	$a + b = 8$ $3a - b = 12$	**2**	$c + d = 7$ $4c - d = 8$
3	$e + f = 5$ $4e - f = 5$	**4**	$g + h = 6$ $5g - h = 12$
5	$j + k = 7$ $4j - k = 23$	**6**	$l + m = 9$ $2l - m = 6$
7	$n + p = 9$ $4n - p = 1$	**8**	$q + r = 9$ $10q - r = 2$
9	$s + t = 8$ $5s - t = 16$	**10**	$u + v = 15$ $2u - v = 6$
11	$3a + 2b = 8$ $2a - 2b = 2$	**12**	$c + 4d = 16$ $5c - 4d = 8$
13	$e + 2f = 8$ $5e - 2f = 4$	**14**	$3g + 4h = 21$ $9g - 4h = 15$
15	$3j + 4k = 23$ $2j - 4k = 2$	**16**	$3l + 2m = 14$ $5l - 2m = 2$
17	$n + 4p = 13$ $12n - 4p = 0$	**18**	$n + 6p = 19$ $3n - 6p = -15$
19	$r + 6s = 11$ $r - 6s = -1$	**20**	$t + 3u = 22$ $7t - 3u = -14$

In Exercise 7.1, in each case, one variable was eliminated by *addition*. In the next two examples one variable is eliminated by *subtraction*.

Worked examples

(i) Solve these simultaneous equations by eliminating by subtraction.

$$5a + 2b = 16 \qquad \text{equation 1}$$
$$3a + 2b = 12 \qquad \text{equation 2}$$

Subtract equation 2 from equation 1:

$$5a + 2b = 16$$
$$\underline{3a + 2b = 12}$$
$$2a \qquad = 4$$

Therefore $a = 2$.

Substitute $a = 2$ in equation 1:

$$5a + 2b = 16$$
$$10 + 2b = 16$$
$$2b = 16 - 10$$
$$2b = 6$$
$$b = 3$$

Check in equation 2; substitute $a = 2$, $b = 3$:

$$3a + 2b = 12$$
$$6 + 6 = 12 \ \checkmark$$

....

(ii) Solve these simultaneous equations by eliminating by subtraction.

$$4c - 3d = 14 \qquad \text{equation 1}$$
$$c - 3d = -1 \qquad \text{equation 2}$$

Subtract equation 2 from equation 1:

$$4c - 3d = 14$$
$$\underline{c - 3d = -1}$$
$$3c \qquad = 15$$

Note: $14 - (-1) = 15$

Therefore $c = 5$.

Substitute $c = 5$ in equation 1:

$$4c - 3d = 14$$
$$20 - 3d = 14$$
$$-3d = 14 - 20$$
$$-3d = -6$$
$$d = 2$$

Check in equation 2; substitute $c = 5$, $d = 2$:

$$c - 3d = -1$$
$$5 - 6 = -1 \ \checkmark$$

EXERCISE 7.2

Solve each of these pairs of simultaneous equations by elimination.

1 $3a + 2b = 10$
   $2a + 2b = 8$

2 $3c + 4d = 13$
   $c + 4d = 7$

3 $5e - 2f = 4$
   $2e - 2f = -2$

4 $4g - 2h = 8$
   $g - 2h = -1$

5 $j - k = 1$
   $2j - k = 3$

6 $l - 2m = -5$
   $3l - 2m = -3$

7 $2n - p = 0$
   $n - p = -2$

8 $3q + 2r = 14$
   $q + 2r = 6$

9 $s + t = 8$
   $5s + t = 28$

10 $2u + v = 6$
    $3u + v = 7$

11 $3a + 2b = 10$
    $3a - b = 4$

12 $2c - d = -1$
    $2c + 3d = 11$

13 $4e - 2f = 8$
    $4e + 3f = 18$

14 $g + h = 3$
    $g + 4h = 9$

15 $j + 2k = 8$
    $j - 3k = -7$

16 $4l + m = 20$
    $4l + 2m = 24$

17 $2n + 3p = 11$
    $2n - 2p = -4$

18 $3r - s = -1$
    $3r - 2s = -8$

19 $t + u = 11$
    $t + 3u = 29$

20 $4t + 5u = 49$
    $4t + u = 29$

Worked example

Solve these simultaneous equations.

$x + 2y = 7$ equation 1
$3x + y = 11$ equation 2

In this case, simply adding or subtracting the equations will not result in the elimination of either x or y. An extra process is needed.

Remember that if you multiply all the terms of an equation by the same number, it does not affect their equality. For example, if you multiply $y = x$ throughout by 2 you get the equation $2y = 2x$. This is equivalent to $y = x$.

Multiply equation 1 throughout by 3, and call the result equation 3.

$x + 2y = 7$ equation 1
$\times 3$ $3x + 6y = 21$ equation 3

Now replace equation 1 by equation 3 in the pair of simultaneous equations.

$3x + 6y = 21$ equation 3
$3x + y = 11$ equation 2

Subtract equation 2 from equation 3 to eliminate x:

$$3x + 6y = 21$$
$$\underline{3x + y = 11}$$
$$5y = 10$$

Therefore $y = 2$.

Substitute $y = 2$ in equation 1:

$$x + 2y = 7$$
$$x + 4 = 7$$
$$x = 7 - 4$$
$$= 3$$

Check by substituting $x = 3$, $y = 2$ in equation 2:

$$3x + y = 11$$
$$9 + 2 = 11 \checkmark$$

EXERCISE 7.3

Solve each of these pairs of simultaneous equations by elimination.

1 $a + 3b = 5$
    $3a + 2b = 8$

2 $b + 3c = 7$
    $2b + c = 4$

3 $2d + e = 7$
    $3d + 2e = 12$

4 $3f + g = 11$
    $2f + 3g = 12$

5 $2h - j = 3$
    $3h + 2j = 8$

6 $2k - 2l = -2$
    $3k + l = 5$

7 $3m - 4n = -14$
    $2m + 2n = 14$

8 $p + q = 7$
    $2p - 3q = -6$

9 $r + 2s = 1$
    $3r - s = -4$

10 $2t + u = 1$
    $3t - 2u = 12$

EXERCISE 7.4

Form a pair of simultaneous equations for each of these solutions.

1 $a = 2, b = 1$

2 $c = 3, d = 2$

3 $e = 2, f = 3$

4 $g = 5, h = 2$

5 $j = 7, k = 1$

6 $l = -1, m = 2$

7 $n = 3, p = -2$

8 $q = 5, r = -3$

9 $s = -2, t = -3$

10 $u = 1, v = -1$

Practical examples of using simultaneous equations

The lengths of the sides of this rectangle are expressed algebraically.

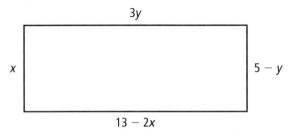

Because opposite sides of a rectangle are the same length, two equations can be formed:

$$3y = 13 - 2x \quad \text{and} \quad x = 5 - y$$

These form a pair of simultaneous equations in x and y. If we solve these equations, we can work out the lengths of the sides of the rectangle.

First rearrange the equations to form a pair.

$$2x + 3y = 13 \qquad \text{equation 1}$$
$$x + y = 5 \qquad \text{equation 2}$$

Multiply equation 2 by 2 and call this equation 3:

$$2x + 3y = 13 \qquad \text{equation 1}$$
$$2x + 2y = 10 \qquad \text{equation 3}$$

Subtract equation 3 from equation 1:

$$2x + 3y = 13$$
$$\underline{2x + 2y = 10}$$
$$y = 3$$

Substitute $y = 3$ in equation 1:

$$2x + 3y = 13$$
$$2x + 9 = 13$$
$$2x = 13 - 9$$
$$= 4$$
$$x = 2$$

Check by substituting $x = 2$, $y = 3$ in equation 2:

$$x + y = 5$$
$$2 + 3 = 5 \ \checkmark$$

In the original diagram, the lengths of the sides were:

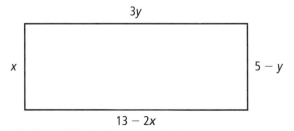

By substitution, the lengths of the sides are:

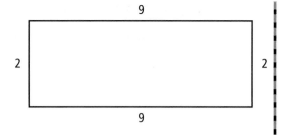

Worked example

Find the lengths of the sides of this rectangle.

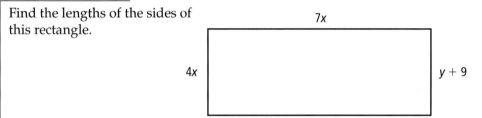

First, form two equations:

$$4x = y + 9 \qquad 7x = y + 18$$

Rearrange the equations to give:

$$4x - y = 9 \qquad \text{equation 1}$$
$$7x - y = 18 \qquad \text{equation 2}$$

Subtract equation 1 from equation 2:

$$7x - y = 18$$
$$4x - y = 9$$
$$\overline{3x \qquad = 9}$$

Therefore $x = 3$.

Substitute $x = 3$ in equation 1:

$$4x - y = 9$$
$$12 - y = 9$$
$$12 - 9 = y$$
$$3 = y$$

Check by substituting $x = 3$, $y = 3$ in equation 2:

$$7x - y = 18$$
$$21 - 3 = 18 \ \checkmark$$

The lengths of the sides are:

EXERCISE 7.5

Copy the following diagrams. By forming and solving a pair of simultaneous equations, find the lengths of the sides of each of the rectangles.

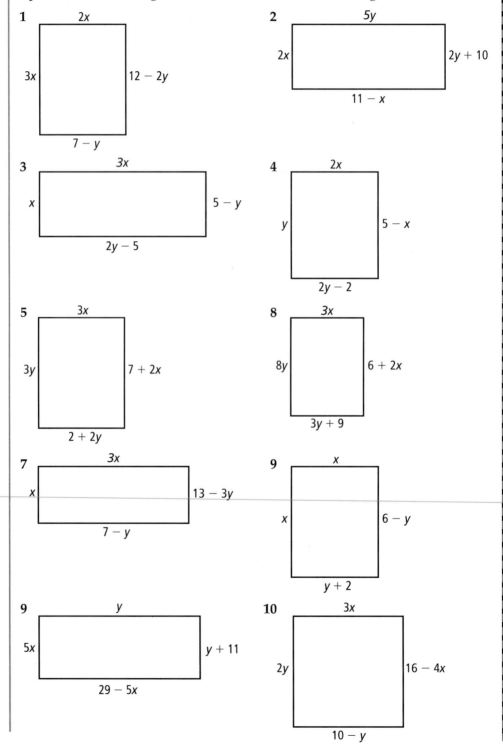

1

2x

3x | 12 − 2y

7 − y

2

5y

2x | 2y + 10

11 − x

3

3x

x | 5 − y

2y − 5

4

2x

y | 5 − x

2y − 2

5

3x

3y | 7 + 2x

2 + 2y

8

3x

8y | 6 + 2x

3y + 9

7

3x

x | 13 − 3y

7 − y

9

x

x | 6 − y

y + 2

9

y

5x | y + 11

29 − 5x

10

3x

2y | 16 − 4x

10 − y

Problem solving using simultaneous equations

Worked example

The sum of two numbers is 27, and their difference is 9. By forming two equations and solving them, find the two numbers.

First, call the numbers x and y and use the information given to form a pair of simultaneous equations.

$$x + y = 27 \qquad \text{equation 1}$$
$$x - y = 9 \qquad \text{equation 2}$$

Adding the equations gives:

$$
\begin{aligned}
x + y &= 27 \\
\underline{x - y} &= \underline{9} \\
2x &= 36 \\
x &= 18
\end{aligned}
$$

Substitute $x = 18$ in equation 1:

$$
\begin{aligned}
x + y &= 27 \\
18 + y &= 27 \\
y &= 27 - 18 \\
y &= 9
\end{aligned}
$$

Check by substituting $x = 18$, $y = 9$ into equation 2:

$$
\begin{aligned}
x - y &= 9 \\
18 - 9 &= 9 \ \checkmark
\end{aligned}
$$

The two numbers are 18 and 9.

EXERCISE 7.6

For each of the following problems, form two equations and solve them to find the two numbers.

1   The sum of two numbers is 10, and their difference is 2.
2   The sum of two numbers is 26, and their difference is 2.
3   The sum of two numbers is 50, and their difference is 18.
4   The sum of two numbers is 12, and their difference is 8.
5   The sum of two numbers is 60, and half their difference is 10.
6–10 Make up five questions of this kind. Ask a friend to try to solve them.

8 Shape, space and measures 4

Conversion graphs, distance–time graphs, and travel graphs

Conversion graphs

1 pound sterling (£) can be converted (changed) to 1.8 US dollars ($). Here is a straight-line graph which can be used to convert dollars to pounds or pounds to dollars.

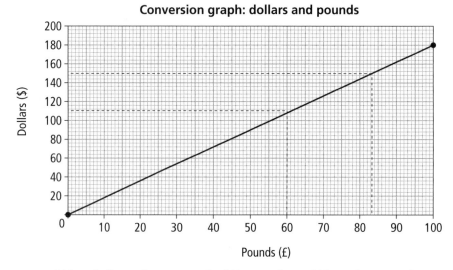

Conversion graph: dollars and pounds

To convert £60 to dollars, draw a vertical line up from £60 on the pounds axis until it reaches the graph line. Then draw a horizontal line across from this graph line to meet the dollars axis at approximately $110.

To convert $300 to pounds is more difficult because the dollars scale only goes up to $200. However, you can find the conversion for $150 and then double it to find the amount required.

Draw a horizontal line across from $150 on the dollars axis to meet the graph line and then draw a vertical line down to meet the pounds axis at approximately £83. Therefore $300 is approximately £166.

EXERCISE 8.1

1 Use the graph above to convert these to dollars.
   (a) £40   (b) £75   (c) £350

2 Use the graph above to convert these to pounds.
   (a) $80   (b) $45   (c) $650

EXERCISE 8.2

You will need graph paper for this exercise.

80 km is approximately the same as 50 miles. Draw a conversion graph with kilometres as the *y* axis and miles as the *x* axis. Use your conversion graph to convert the following:

1 70 miles to km

2 40 km to miles

3 20 miles to km

4 65 km to miles

5 240 miles to km

6 420 km to miles

7 The speed limit on motorways in Britain is 70 miles per hour. Convert this to km/h.

8 The speed limit on German motorways is 130 km/h. Convert this to miles per hour.

9 The speed of sound is approximately 1000 km/h. Convert this to miles per hour.

10 Light travels at 186 000 miles per second. Use your conversion graph to convert this to km/s.

EXERCISE 8.3

You will need graph paper for this exercise.

This graph is used to convert temperatures from Celsius to Fahrenheit or from Fahrenheit to Celsius.

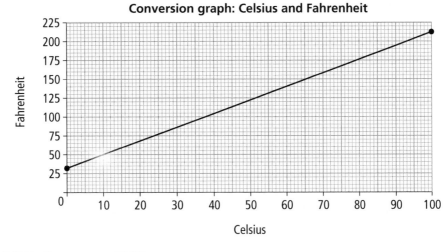

Conversion graph: Celsius and Fahrenheit

0 °C is the same as 32 °F.
100 °C is the same as 212 °F.

Copy the conversion graph and use it to answer the questions.

1 Convert 70 °C to Fahrenheit.

2 Convert 120 °F to Celsius.

3 Convert 40 °C to Fahrenheit.

4 Convert 90 °F to Celsius.

5 Body temperature is 98 °F. Convert this to Celsius.

6 Convert 23 °C to Fahrenheit.

7 The highest recorded air temperature is 56 °C in Iraq. Convert this to Fahrenheit.

8 A thermometer shows a temperature of 100 °F. Convert this to Celsius.

9 By extending your graph, convert 0 °F to Celsius.

10 Convert −40 °F to Celsius.

EXERCISE 8.4

You will need graph paper for this exercise.

An approximate conversion from Celsius to Fahrenheit is given by the formula

$$F = 2C + 30$$

where F is degrees Fahrenheit and C is degrees Celsius.

1   Draw a graph on the same axes as the one in Exercise 8.3.

2   For what Fahrenheit/Celsius temperature do the two graphs give the same conversion value?

EXERCISE 8.5

You will need graph paper for this exercise.

Ayse has a mobile phone. She pays the following tariff per month:

a set charge of €20 and then 5 cents per minute

Her friend, Bella, has a different tariff where she pays 12 cents per minute with no set charge.

The different methods of payment can be compared by looking at graphs that 'convert' the amount of time spent on the phone (minutes) to the cost in €.

Draw two conversion graphs on one grid with the same axes, and use your graphs to find the following charges in one month. Draw your time axis up to 20 hours (1200 minutes).

1 Ayse uses her phone for 300 minutes.

2 Bella uses her phone for 300 minutes.

3 Ayse uses her phone for 2 hours.

4 Bella uses her phone for 6 hours.

5 Ayse is on holiday for a month and does not take her phone.

6 Bella is on holiday for a month and does not take her phone.

7 Ayse uses her phone for 10 hours.

8 Bella uses her phone for 15 hours.

9 At what point should Ayse consider changing to Bella's way of paying?

10 At what point should Bella consider changing to Ayse's way of paying?

Distance–time graphs

In Chapter 2, you used the formulae

$$\text{speed} = \frac{\text{distance}}{\text{time}}$$

$$\text{distance} = \text{speed} \times \text{time}$$

$$\text{time} = \frac{\text{distance}}{\text{speed}}$$

An object travelling at a constant speed can be shown as a straight line on a graph.

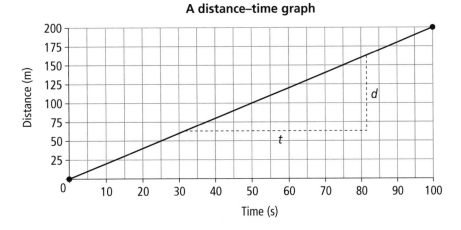

A distance–time graph

The gradient of the graph is found by the formula

$$\text{gradient} = \frac{d}{t}$$

If the distance is in metres and the time in seconds, the units of the gradient are m/s. Therefore the gradient represents the speed of the object.

Worked example

Use the graph on page 51 to find:
(a) how long the object takes to travel 50 m
(b) how far the object travels in 70 s
(c) how far the object travels in 12 minutes.

(a) Reading across to the graph and down to the horizontal axis, we get 25 seconds.
(b) Reading up to the graph and across to the vertical axis, we get 140 m.
(c) Convert 12 minutes into seconds:

$$12 \min = 720 \text{ s}$$

The time axis on the graph only goes up to 100 s, so work out the answer by using a combination:

$$720 \text{ s} = [(70 \times 10) + 20] \text{ s}$$

The distance travelled in 70 s is 140 m (from part **(b)**).
So the distance travelled in 700 s is 1400 m.
Reading from the graph, the distance travelled in 20 s is 40 m.
Therefore the distance travelled in 720 s is (1400 + 40) m = 1440 m.

EXERCISE 8.6

This graph shows an object travelling at 8 m/s (a distance of 80 m in 10 seconds, which is equivalent to 400 m in 50 seconds).

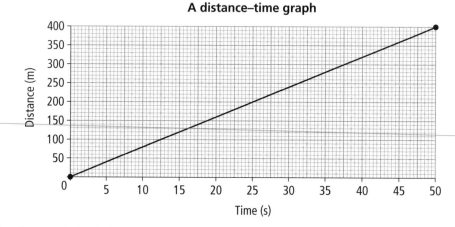

A distance–time graph

Use the graph to find:

1 how long the object takes to travel 50 m

2 how far the object travels in 5 seconds

3 how long the object takes to travel 70 m

4 how far the object travels in 8 seconds

5 how long the object takes to travel 650 m

6   how far the object travels in 1 minute

7   how long the object takes to travel 1 km

8   how far the object travels in 5 minutes

9   how long the object takes to travel 550 m

10   how many metres the object travels in 1 hour.

EXERCISE 8.7

You will need graph paper for this exercise.

A second object travels at 12 m/s (a distance of 120 m in 10 seconds, or 600 m in 50 s). Draw a graph and use it to answer the same questions as in Exercise 8.6 for this object.

Travel graphs

EXERCISE 8.8

You will need squared paper for this exercise.

The graph below shows a family car journey. Copy the graph and use it to answer the questions.

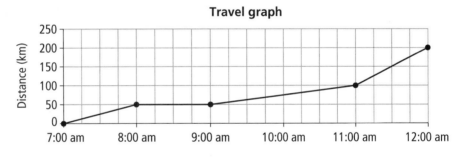

1   What time did the family set out?

2   **(a)** How far did they travel in the first hour?
    (b) What was their average speed in the first hour?

3   What time did they stop for breakfast?

4   How long did they stop for breakfast?

5   How far did they travel between 9.00 am and 11.00 am?

6   What was their average speed during those two hours?

7   The family reached a motorway at 11.00 am. What was their average speed for the next hour?

8   How long did the whole journey take?

9 How far did they travel in total?

10 What was the average speed for the whole journey?

11 A second family sets out on the same journey by train. They leave at 9.30 am and arrive at noon. Show this journey on your graph, assuming the train travels at a constant speed.

12 What was the average speed of the train?

EXERCISE 8.9

You will need squared paper for this exercise.

1 A salesman leaves home at 0800 and travels for $1\frac{1}{2}$ hours at an average speed of 60 km/h. He then stops for 30 minutes. He continues for 2 more hours at 50 km/h and stops for 1 hour. He then returns home and arrives home at 1600.
(a) Show this in a travel graph.
(b) Calculate the salesman's average speed on the return journey.

2 A train leaves a station at 0730. It travels for 1 hour 30 minutes at 100 km/h and then stops for 15 minutes. It travels a further 200 km at 100 km/h and then stops for 30 minutes. It then does the return journey non-stop at 100 km/h.
(a) Draw a graph of the journey.
(b) When does the train arrive back at the station?

3 This graph shows a boy's journey by cycle. Use it to answer the questions below.

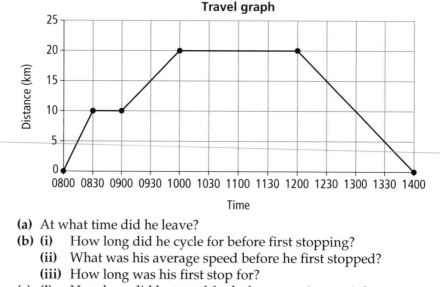

(a) At what time did he leave?
(b) (i)   How long did he cycle for before first stopping?
    (ii) What was his average speed before he first stopped?
    (iii) How long was his first stop for?
(c) (i)   How long did he travel for before stopping again?
    (ii) How far had he travelled during this time?
    (iii) What was his average speed for this part of the journey?
(d) What does the graph show from noon to 1400?
(e) What was the boy's average speed for his return journey?
(f) What was his average speed for the day's total journey?

Shape, space and measures 5

Trigonometry – the tangent ratio

Trigonometry and the trigonometric ratios developed from the ancient study of the stars. The study of right-angled triangles probably originated with the Egyptians and the Babylonians, who used them extensively in construction and engineering.

The trigonometric ratios, one of which is introduced in this chapter, were set out by Hipparchos of Rhodes about 150 BC.

Trigonometry was used extensively in navigation at sea, particularly in the sailing ships of the eighteenth and nineteenth centuries.

Mohammad Abu'l-Wafa al'Buzjani was born in Buzjan in Iran in AD 940 and died in 998 in Baghdad, which was a great centre of learning. He was the first to use the tangent function, and he compiled a set of tables of sine, cosine and tangent accurate to 8 decimal places. He used these in astronomy.

The tangent ratio

The sides of a right-angled triangle have names. You already know that the longest side is called the **hypotenuse**. It is always opposite the right angle. The names of the other two sides depend on their position in relation to a specific chosen angle. They are **opposite** or **adjacent** (next) to one of the other angles chosen in the right-angled triangle, as shown in the diagrams.

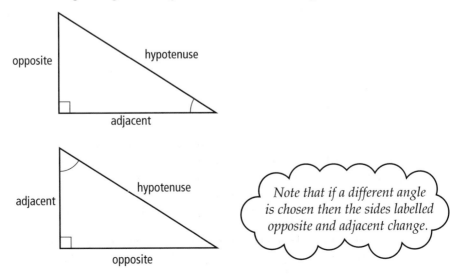

Note that if a different angle is chosen then the sides labelled opposite and adjacent change.

EXERCISE 9.1

Draw triangles similar to the ones below. On each triangle, mark the hypotenuse, the side opposite and the side adjacent to the marked angle.

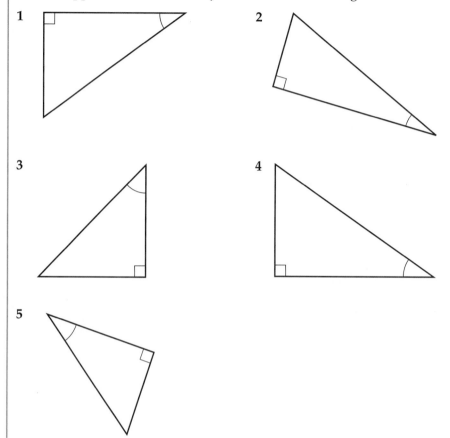

Hipparchos noticed that when he divided the length of the opposite side by the length of the adjacent side in a right-angled triangle, the ratio was constant for a fixed angle, no matter what size the triangle was.

The ratio of opposite to adjacent for an angle in a right-angled triangle is called the **tangent ratio**.

EXERCISE 9.2

You will need a protractor and a calculator for this exercise.

1   (a) Draw a right-angled triangle with a base angle of 35° similar to this one.

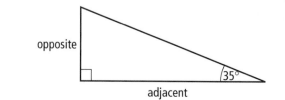

(b) Measure the lengths of the opposite and adjacent sides.

(c) Find the ratio of the lengths $\dfrac{\text{opposite}}{\text{adjacent}}$ for the triangle.

(d) Draw four other different-sized right-angled triangles, but still each with a base angle of 35°.

(e) For each of the triangles drawn in part **(d)**, calculate the ratio of the lengths $\dfrac{\text{opposite}}{\text{adjacent}}$. What do you notice about the results?

2   Repeat question 1 for a right-angled triangle with a base angle of 60°.

EXERCISE 9.3

You will need a protractor and a calculator for this exercise.

1   **(a)** Draw a right-angled triangle with base 10 cm and base angle 20°.

(b) Find the ratio of the lengths $\dfrac{\text{opposite}}{\text{adjacent}}$.

(c) Copy this table and enter your results in the first row.

Angle	Length of opposite side	Length of adjacent side	Opposite ÷ adjacent
20°		10 cm	
30°		10 cm	
40°		10 cm	
50°		10 cm	
60°		10 cm	
70°		10 cm	

(d) Draw right-angled triangles with base 10 cm and base angles of 30°, 40°, 50°, etc., and enter your results in the rest of the table.

2   Your calculator has a [tan] button which allows you to find the tangent ratio for any angle.

Press [tan] then 20 (or 20 and then [tan]). The calculator should give an answer of 0.36397 (to 5 dp). How does this compare with the first number in the final column of your table from question 1?

3   **(a)** Use your calculator to check the accuracy of the rest of the results in the final column of your table.

(b) Your results table is unlikely to be exactly correct. Why might this be?

EXERCISE 9.4

You will need a calculator for this exercise.

Copy these diagrams. Use a calculator to find the tangent of the angle marked in each of these right-angled triangles. Remember tangent $= \dfrac{\text{opposite}}{\text{adjacent}}$.

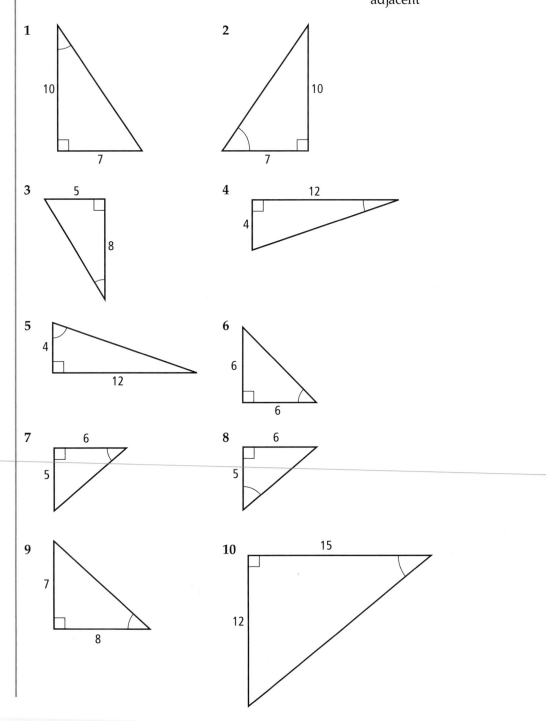

Once the tangent ratio has been calculated, it is then possible to calculate the size of the angle.

$$\tan a = \frac{\text{opposite}}{\text{adjacent}}$$

The tangent of angle a is abbreviated to tan a.

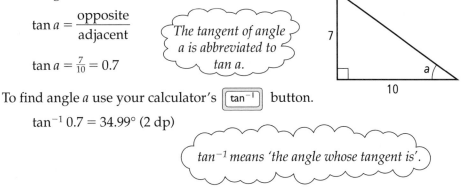

$$\tan a = \tfrac{7}{10} = 0.7$$

To find angle *a* use your calculator's $\boxed{\tan^{-1}}$ button.

$$\tan^{-1} 0.7 = 34.99° \text{ (2 dp)}$$

$\tan^{-1}$ means 'the angle whose tangent is'.

EXERCISE 9.5

Using the $\tan^{-1}$ button of your calculator, calculate the size of each of the marked angles in the triangles of Exercise 9.4.

We can also use the tangent ratio to find the lengths of sides in a right-angled triangle.

Look at the formula that we have already used,

tangent of an angle $= \dfrac{\text{length of the opposite side}}{\text{length of the adjacent side}}$

or, more simply,

$\tan A = \dfrac{\text{opposite}}{\text{adjacent}}$

We can rearrange the formula to make the 'opposite' the subject of the formula:

$$\tan A \times \text{adjacent} = \text{opposite}$$

Similarly, we can make the 'adjacent' the subject:

$$\text{adjacent} = \frac{\text{opposite}}{\tan A}$$

Worked examples

(i) For this right-angled triangle, find the length of the side marked *x*.

$$\tan 35° = \frac{x}{25}$$
$$x = 25 \times \tan 35°$$
$$= 17.5 \text{ (1 dp)}$$

Therefore *x* = 17.5 cm.

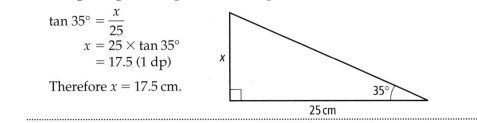

(ii) For this right-angled triangle, find the length of the side marked y.

$$\tan 62° = \frac{y}{12}$$

$$y = 12 \times \tan 62°$$

$$= 22.6 \text{ (1 dp)}$$

Therefore $y = 22.6$ cm.

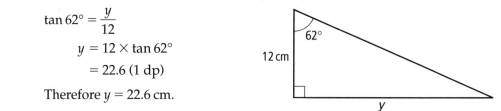

62°

12 cm

y

EXERCISE 9.6

For each diagram, calculate the length of the side marked x.

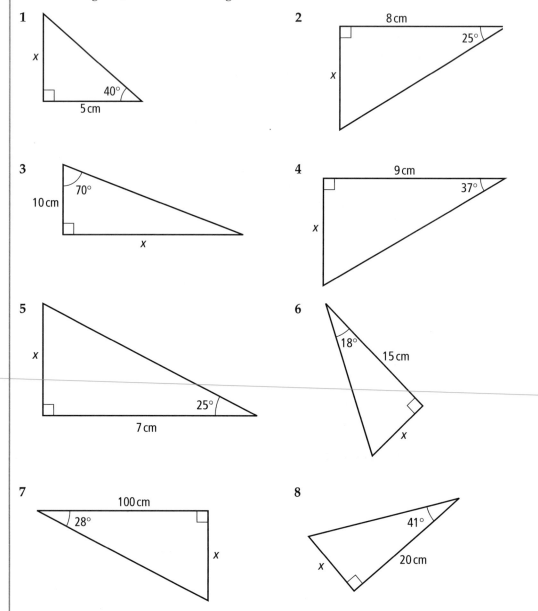

1

x

40°

5 cm

2

8 cm

25°

x

3

70°

10 cm

x

4

9 cm

37°

x

5

x

25°

7 cm

6

18°

15 cm

x

7

100 cm

28°

x

8

41°

20 cm

x

9

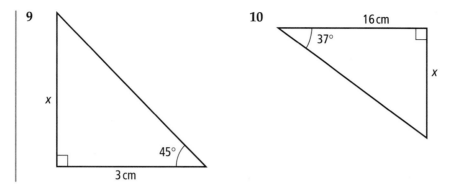

10

Worked examples

(i) Find the length of the side marked a in this diagram.

$$\tan 35° = \frac{12}{a}$$

$$a \times \tan 35° = 12$$

$$a = \frac{12}{\tan 35°}$$

$$= 17.1 \text{ (1 dp)}$$

Therefore $a = 17.1$ cm.

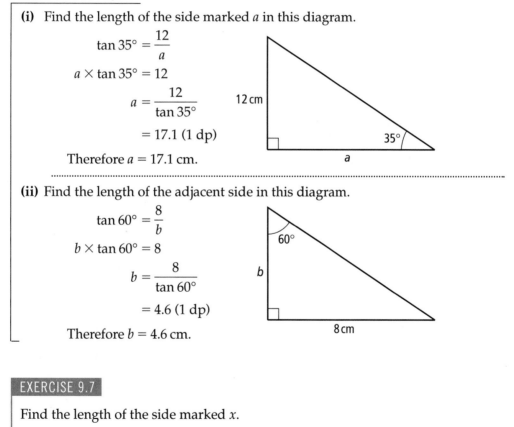

(ii) Find the length of the adjacent side in this diagram.

$$\tan 60° = \frac{8}{b}$$

$$b \times \tan 60° = 8$$

$$b = \frac{8}{\tan 60°}$$

$$= 4.6 \text{ (1 dp)}$$

Therefore $b = 4.6$ cm.

EXERCISE 9.7

Find the length of the side marked x.

1

2

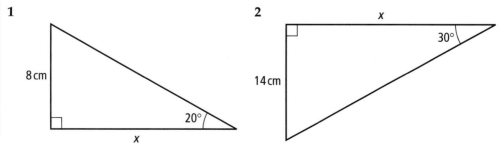

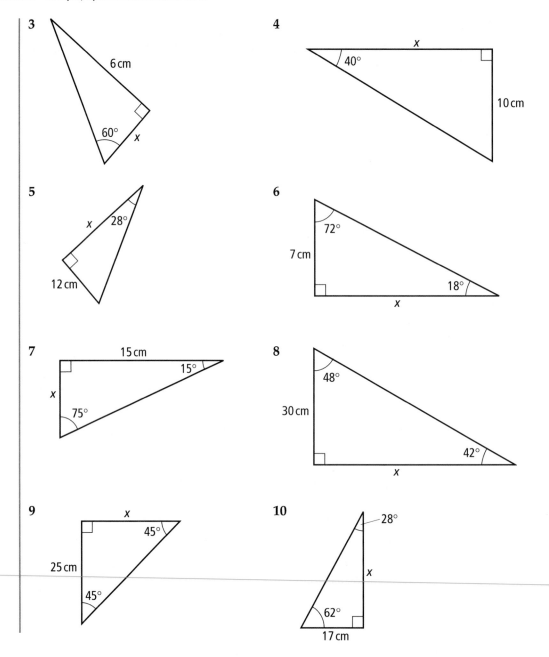

3

6 cm

60° x

4

x

40°

10 cm

5

x 28°

12 cm

6

72°

7 cm

18°

x

7

15 cm

15°

x

75°

8

48°

30 cm

42°

x

9

x

45°

25 cm

45°

10

28°

x

62°

17 cm

Investigation

Equipment needed: tape measure, clinometer (to measure angles)

1 Go outside and find a tall object (for example, a building or a tree).
2 Measure the horizontal distance d between you and the object.
3 Measure the angle of elevation a from you to the top of the object (see the diagram).

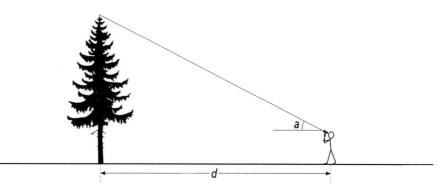

4 Repeat the process several times for different values of d.
5 Record your results in a table like this one.

Object	Result	Distance d	Angle a	Height of object	Average height
Tree	1				
	2				
	3				
	4				

6 Using trigonometry, use your values of d and a to calculate the height of the object.
7 Why do you need to add your own height to the final result, to get a true value for the height of the object?
8 Repeat the experiment for other objects.

ICT activity

In this activity you will be using a spreadsheet to produce a conversion graph between two currencies.

- Choose a holiday destination of your choice.
- Using the internet or a newspaper as a resource, find the exchange rate between the currency of the country you are in and the currency of the country you wish to travel to for your holiday. (For example, if you live in South Africa and wish to travel to the UK, you would look up the exchange rate between the South African rand and pounds sterling.)
- Using the exchange rate, draw up a conversion table in your spreadsheet.
- Using the graphing facility of the spreadsheet, plot a conversion graph between the two currencies.

Summary

At the end of this section you should know:
* how to write large numbers in standard form
* * how to write numbers between 0 and 1 in standard form using a negative index
* how to enter numbers into a calculator in standard form
* how to solve simultaneous equations by elimination
* how to form simultaneous equations from a problem and solve them to find the solution
* what is meant by a conversion graph
* how to construct a conversion graph in order to convert a quantity in one unit into another unit
* how to read information from distance–time graphs (travel graphs)
* how to construct a travel graph from information given
* that the tangent ratio is part of trigonometry
* that the tangent ratio gives the relationship between an angle and the opposite and adjacent sides of a right-angled triangle
* how to solve problems involving the tangent ratio
* how to use the 'tan' button on your calculator to solve problems involving the tangent ratio
* how to use the 'tan^{-1}' function on your calculator to calculate the size of an angle.

Review 2A

1 Write each of these in standard form.
   (a) 5 000 000   (b) 23 million   (c) 0.45×10^5

2 Multiply each of these and give your answer in standard form.
   (a) $60\,000 \times 2000$ (b) $4\,000\,000 \times 3000$ (c) $(5000)^2$

3 Using a calculator, write the answer to each of these calculations in standard form.
   (a) $(3.4 \times 10^5) \times (18 \times 10^3)$
   (b) $(5.6 \times 10^4) \times (2.1 \times 10^4)$
   (c) $(2.8 \times 10^4)^2$

* 4 Write each of these in standard form.
   (a) 0.0008   (b) 0.000 004 16   (c) 0.000 72

5 Solve each of these pairs of simultaneous equations.
   (a) $3x + 2y = 13$ (b) $2p + 5q = 9$
       $5x - 2y = 11$ $3p + 5q = 11$

* **6** Form a pair of simultaneous equations and solve them to find:
  (a) the values of p and q
  (b) the lengths of the sides of the rectangle.

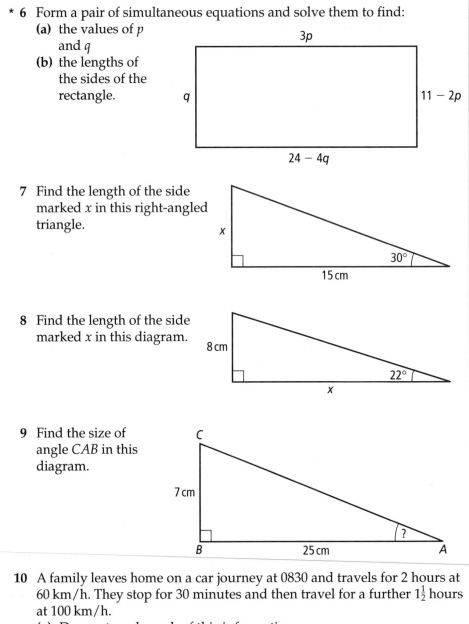

7 Find the length of the side marked x in this right-angled triangle.

8 Find the length of the side marked x in this diagram.

9 Find the size of angle CAB in this diagram.

10 A family leaves home on a car journey at 0830 and travels for 2 hours at 60 km/h. They stop for 30 minutes and then travel for a further $1\frac{1}{2}$ hours at 100 km/h.
  (a) Draw a travel graph of this information.
  (b) How far have they travelled in total?
  (c) What is their average speed for the whole journey?

Review 2B

1 Write each of these in standard form.
   (a) 17 million
   (b) $\frac{3}{4}$ million
   (c) 8 billion

2 Multiply each of these and give your answer in standard form.
   (a) 400×5000
   (b) $6\,000\,000 \times 300$
   (c) $(800)^2$

3 Using a calculator, write the answer to each of these calculations in standard form.
   (a) $(4.1 \times 10^4) \times (1.7 \times 10^3)$
   (b) $(5.08 \times 10^3)^2$
   (c) $(4.9 \times 10^6) \div (3.2 \times 10^2)$

* 4 Write each of these in standard form.
   (a) 0.0006
   (b) 0.000 073
   (c) $\frac{8}{100\,000}$

5 Solve each of these pairs of simultaneous equations.
   (a) $3p + 4q = 35$
       $3p - 4q = -5$
   (b) $a + b = 7$
       $3a + 2b = 17$

* 6 From the information given in this rectangle:
   (a) construct two simultaneous equations
   (b) solve the simultaneous equations to find the values of p and q
   (c) calculate the length of the sides of the rectangle.

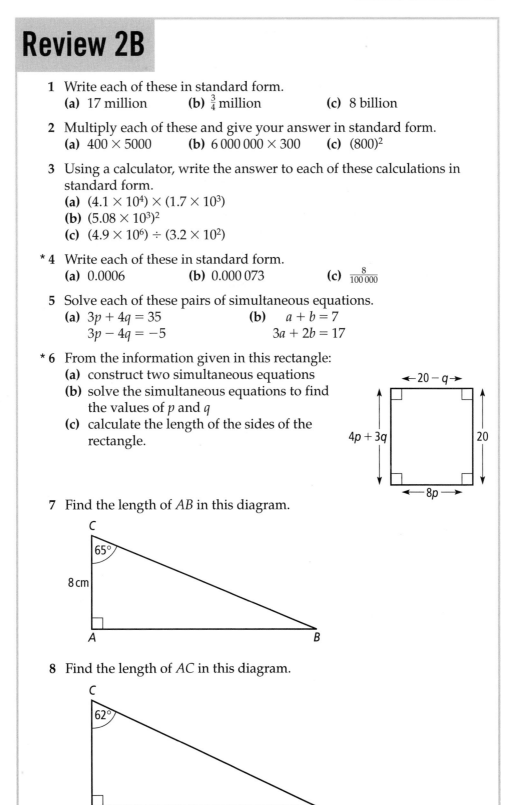

7 Find the length of AB in this diagram.

8 Find the length of AC in this diagram.

9 Find the size of the angle *ACB* in this diagram.

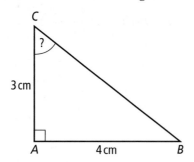

10 The electricity bill for a family is calculated as follows: a basic fee of €50 for 3 months plus €15 for each 100 units used.

(a) Draw a conversion graph and find the total cost when 2500 units of electricity are used.

(b) A different tariff charges 20 cents per unit with no basic fee. At which point are the charges the same for both tariffs?

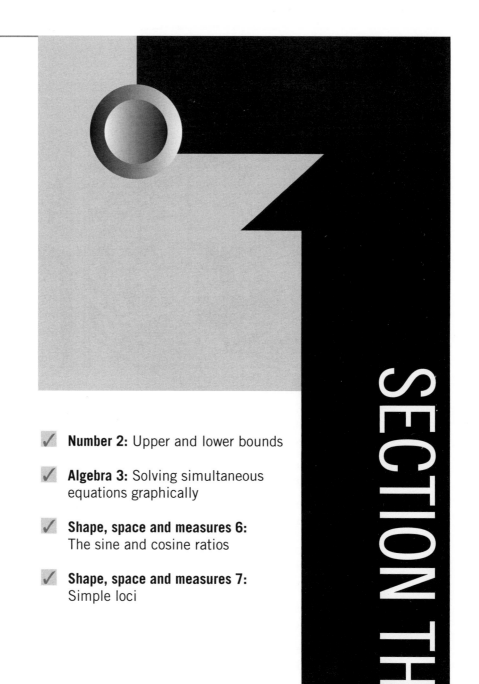

SECTION THREE

Number 2

Upper and lower bounds

UPPER AND LOWER LIMITS
To use this ride you must
be over 14 years old,
and at least 150 cm tall
and not taller than
2 m.

Revision

In Book 2, Chapter 11, we looked at inequality signs.
The basic inequality symbols are $<$ and $>$.

$x < y$ means x **is less than** y.
$x > y$ means x **is greater than** y.

So a sentence such as 'Everyone in a class of pupils is less than 13 years old'
could be expressed as:

$a < 13$ where a is the age of pupils, in years

Two more symbols $\leqslant$ and $\geqslant$ are formed by putting part of an equals sign under
the inequality symbol.

$x \leqslant y$ means x **is less than or equal to** y.
$x \geqslant y$ means x **is greater than or equal to** y.

So a sentence such as 'This nursery school takes children who are four years old
or more' could be expressed as:

$a \geqslant 4$ where a is the age of children, in years

The following pairs of expressions (inequalities) mean the same:

$x < y$ (x is less than y)   and $y > x$ (y is greater than x)
$x \leqslant y$ (x is less than or equal to y)   and $y \geqslant x$ (y is greater than or equal to x)

So $5 < x$ is usually written as $x > 5$.

Another symbol used is $\neq$, which means *is not equal to*.

$x \neq 5$ means x **is not equal to** 5.

EXERCISE 11.1

Revision
Rewrite the following using the symbols $\neq$, $>$, $\geq$, $<$ or $\leq$ as appropriate.

1 *a* is less than 9
2 *b* is greater than 8
3 *c* is greater than or equal to 7
4 *d* is less than or equal to 12
5 *e* is not equal to 5
6 *f* is at least 30
7 *g* is at most 15
8 *h* is 7
9 6 is less than *i*
10 10 is more than *j*

In Book 2 you also learned how to use a number line to show an inequality.

The inequality $x \geq 5$ can be shown on a number line like this:

(All values are included, not just whole numbers.)

The inequality $x < 7$ is shown on a number line like this:

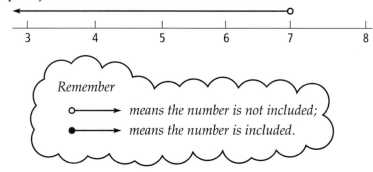

Remember

○———▶ *means the number is not included;*

●———▶ *means the number is included.*

EXERCISE 11.2

Revision
Show each of these inequalities on a number line.

1 $a \geq 5$ 2 $b \leq 8$
3 $c > 6$ 4 $d < 4$
5 $8 \leq e$ 6 $9 \geq f$
7 $6 < g$ 8 $4 > h$
9 $i > 0.5$ 10 $j < 3.5$

In Book 2 you also learned how to combine two inequalities. For example,

$7 < p < 11$ means that p is greater than 7 but less than 11
$7 \leqslant q \leqslant 11$ means that q is greater than or equal to 7 but less than or equal to 11

These two inequalities are shown on number lines as follows:

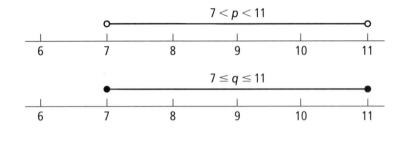

EXERCISE 11.3

Revision
Represent each of these inequalities on a number line.

1	$5 < a < 9$	**2**	$4 \geqslant b \geqslant 1$
3	$8 \leqslant c \leqslant 12$	**4**	$7 > d > 2$
5	$4 < e \leqslant 7$	**6**	$6 \geqslant f > 4$
7	$-6 < g < -2$	**8**	$-4 \geqslant h \geqslant -6$
9	$-3 \leqslant i < 3$	**10**	$5 > j \geqslant 0$

EXERCISE 11.4

Revision
Write down the inequality shown by each of these number lines, using the given letter for the unknown.

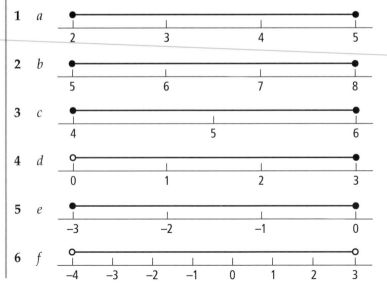

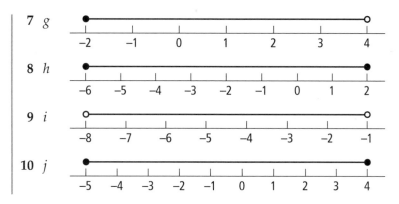

Accuracy

Numbers can be written to different **degrees of accuracy**. For example, if the number of spectators at a football match was 12 836, then you might want to round this to a more convenient number.

Rounded to the nearest 10, 12 836 is 12 840
Rounded to the nearest 100, 12 836 is 12 800
Rounded to the nearest 1000, 12 836 is 13 000

Rounding the number to the nearest 10, nearest 100 or nearest 1000 gives a different degree of accuracy.

The numbers 4, 4.0 and 4.00 appear to represent the same number but they may not. This is because they are written to different degrees of accuracy.

4 is written to 0 decimal places. At this degree of accuracy, any number from 3.5 up to *but not including* 4.5 is rounded to 4. On a number line this is represented as:

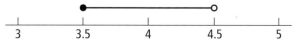

As an inequality, where x represents the number, it is expressed as

$3.5 \leqslant x < 4.5$

In this example, we call 3.5 the **lower bound** of 4 and 4.5 the **upper bound**.

4.0 is written to one decimal place. At this degree of accuracy, numbers from 3.95 up to but not including 4.05 are rounded to 4.0. This therefore represents a much smaller range of numbers than the range of those that are rounded to 4.

Similarly, the range of numbers rounded to 4.00 is even smaller, as shown on this number line:

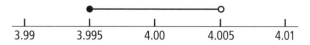

Worked example

A girl's height is given as 162 cm to the nearest centimetre.

(a) Write down the lower and upper bounds within which her height can lie.
(b) Represent this range of numbers on a number line.
(c) If the girl's height is h cm, express this range as an inequality.

(a) Lower bound = 161.5 cm
     Upper bound = 162.5 cm

(b)

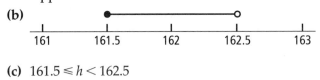

(c) $161.5 \leqslant h < 162.5$

EXERCISE 11.5

Each of the numbers below is shown to the nearest whole number. For each number:

(a) give the upper and lower bounds
(b) using x as the number, show the range of its possible values as an inequality
(c) show the inequality on a number line.

1 8	**2** 45	**3** 156	**4** 200	**5** 3
6 1	**7** −8	**8** −20	**9** −1	**10** 0

EXERCISE 11.6

Each of the numbers below is correct to the given number of decimal places. For each number:

(a) give the upper and lower bounds
(b) using x as the number, show the range of its possible values as an inequality.

1 4.6   (1 dp)

2 8.3   (1 dp)

3 17.5   (1 dp)

4 6.2   (1 dp)

5 0.8   (1 dp)

6 3.0   (1 dp)

7 2.0   (1 dp)

8 4.15   (2 dp)

9 7.38   (2 dp)

10 0.01   (2 dp)

EXERCISE 11.7

1 At a school sports day the shortest time taken to run the 100 m is given as 12.6 seconds, accurate to 0.1 seconds. Illustrate the upper and lower bounds on a number line.

2 The shortest time taken to run the 1500 m is given as 5 minutes 18 seconds, accurate to 1 second. Using t as the time, show the range of possible values as an inequality.

3 The capacity of a pool is given as 5000 litres, correct to 1 significant figure. Illustrate the upper and lower bounds on a number line.

4 The mass of a sack of carrots is given as 12 kg, to the nearest 100 g. Illustrate the upper and lower bounds on a number line.

5 A field measures 300 m by 240 m, to the nearest 10 m. Illustrate the upper and lower bounds of the length and width of the field on number lines.

6 Frances and Daniel are playing with some balance scales. Daniel wants to find the total mass of ten of his toy cars. The smallest weight he can find to use in balancing the scales is 50 g. When Daniel places 600 g in weights, the scale falls, but not when he has 550 g. Illustrate on a number line the upper and lower bounds for the total mass of the cars.

7 Daniel's sister Frances finds some smaller 10 g weights to use in trying to find the total mass of the ten cars. She finds that the scale falls when she has 580 g but not when she has 570 g. Illustrate on a number line the upper and lower bounds for the total mass of the cars.

Questions 8, 9 and 10 show the upper and lower bounds for measurements of time, height and distance at a school sports day. Write suitable questions to which they could be the answer.

8 $24 \leqslant t < 25$

9 $165 \leqslant h < 166$

10 $9.8 \leqslant d < 9.9$

Algebra 3

Solving simultaneous equations graphically

In Chapter 7 of this book you learned how to solve simultaneous equations. This was a way of finding one solution that satisfies two equations involving the same two unknowns (variables). For example, to solve the simultaneous equations

$$x + 3y = 6 \qquad \text{equation 1}$$
$$x + y = 2 \qquad \text{equation 2}$$

First subtract equation 2 from equation 1 so that the variable x is eliminated (removed):

$$\begin{array}{r} x + 3y = 6 \\ \underline{x + y = 2} \\ 2y = 4 \end{array}$$

Therefore $y = 2$.

Substitute $y = 2$ into equation 2:

$$x + 2 = 2$$

Therefore $x = 0$.

Only these two values, $x = 0$, $y = 2$, satisfy both equations.

In Chapter 12 of Book 1 you learned how to plot the graph of a straight line, given its equation.

For example, to plot the graph of the line with equation $y = x - 1$, first choose a few values of x, work out the corresponding y values using the equation and write these in a table of values. This gives you the co-ordinates of a few of the points which lie on the line. Then plot these points on a co-ordinate grid.

x	0	1	2	3	4
y	−1	0	1	2	3

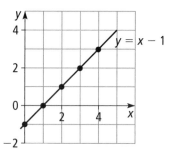

Simultaneous equations can be solved graphically by plotting the lines represented by both equations on the same grid.

Worked example

Solve these simultaneous equations graphically.

$y = x - 5$
$y = -2x + 7$

Find the co-ordinates of some of the points on the line represented by each equation.

$y = x - 5$

x	0	1	2	3	4	5
y	−5	−4	−3	−2	−1	0

$y = -2x + 7$

x	0	1	2	3	4	5
y	7	5	3	1	−1	−3

Plot both lines on the same co-ordinate grid.

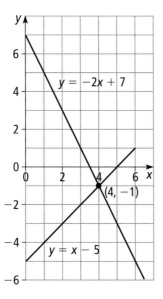

The point where the two lines cross (intersect) is the *only* point that lies on *both* graphs. It therefore represents the solution of the simultaneous equations, $y = x - 5$ and $y = -2x + 7$. So the solution is $x = 4$ and $y = -1$.

EXERCISE 12.1

For each of the following pairs of simultaneous equations:

(a) plot the lines represented by the two equations on the same co-ordinate grid
(b) find the solution to the simultaneous equations.

1 $y = x + 2$
   $y = 2x - 1$

2 $y = x + 1$
   $y = \frac{1}{2}x + 2$

3 $y = x$
   $y = 4$

4 $y = 2x - 3$
   $y = \frac{1}{2}x + 3$

5 $y = \frac{1}{2}x + 2$
   $y = -x + 5$

6 $y = -2$
   $y = -x$

7 $y = -x + 3$
   $y = 4x - 2$

8 $y = 2x + 6$
   $y = -2x - 2$

9 $y = -\frac{1}{2}x + 3$
   $y = -2x - 3$

10 $y = -\frac{1}{2}x + 4$
    $y = -2\frac{1}{2}x + 2$

So far, all the pairs of simultaneous equations you have worked with were in the form $y = mx + c$, which makes it easy to work out a table of values from which to plot points on the line. When equations are not given in this form, you do not need to rearrange them into the form $y = mx + c$. Instead, you can use another method to plot the lines represented by the equations.

Worked example

Solve these simultaneous equations graphically.

$x + 2y = 8$ equation 1
$2x - y = 1$ equation 2

To plot the lines represented by the equations, find where each of the lines intersects the x and y axes.

A line intersects the x axis when $y = 0$.
A line intersects the y axis when $x = 0$.

For equation 1, $x + 2y = 8$,

when $y = 0$, $x = 8$; when $x = 0$, $y = 4$

Therefore the line $x + 2y = 8$ must pass through the points $(8, 0)$ and $(0, 4)$.

For equation 2, $2x - y = 1$,

when $y = 0$, $x = \frac{1}{2}$; when $x = 0$, $y = -1$

Therefore the line $2x - y = 1$ must pass through the points $(\frac{1}{2}, 0)$ and $(0, -1)$.

Plot the lines on a co-ordinate grid.

The solution of the simultaneous equations is the point where the graphs intersect, i.e. $x = 2$ and $y = 3$.

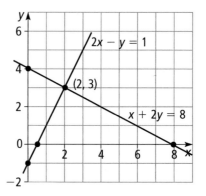

For each of the pairs of simultaneous equations in questions 1–6:

(a) plot the lines represented by the two equations on the same co-ordinate grid

(b) find the solution to the simultaneous equations.

1 $x + y = 5$
   $2x - y = -2$

2 $\frac{1}{2}x - y = 2$
   $2x + y = 3$

3 $x = 3$
   $3x - y = 3$

4 $3x + y = 2$
   $-2x + y = -3$

5 $4y - x = 12$
   $x + y = 8$

6 $y = \frac{1}{2}$
   $y - x = -2$

7 (a) Plot these simultaneous equations on the same co-ordinate grid.

$$y = 2x + 3$$
$$y = 2x - 2$$

   (b) How many solutions are there?
   (c) Explain your answer to part (b).

8 (a) Plot these simultaneous equations on the same co-ordinate grid.

$$y = 3x - 1$$
$$2y = 6x - 2$$

   (b) In your own words describe your graph.
   (c) How many solutions are there?
   (d) Explain your answer to part (c).

9 (a) Plot these simultaneous equations on the same co-ordinate grid.

$$3x - y = 2$$
$$6x - 2y = -4$$

   (b) How many solutions are there?

10 (a) Plot these simultaneous equations on the same co-ordinate grid.

$$\frac{1}{3}x - y = 2$$
$$x - 3y = 6$$

   (b) How many solutions are there?

EXERCISE 12.3

Below are six co-ordinate graphs, six pairs of simultaneous equations and six
solutions. Match each pair of simultaneous equations with its graph and solution.

Co-ordinate graphs

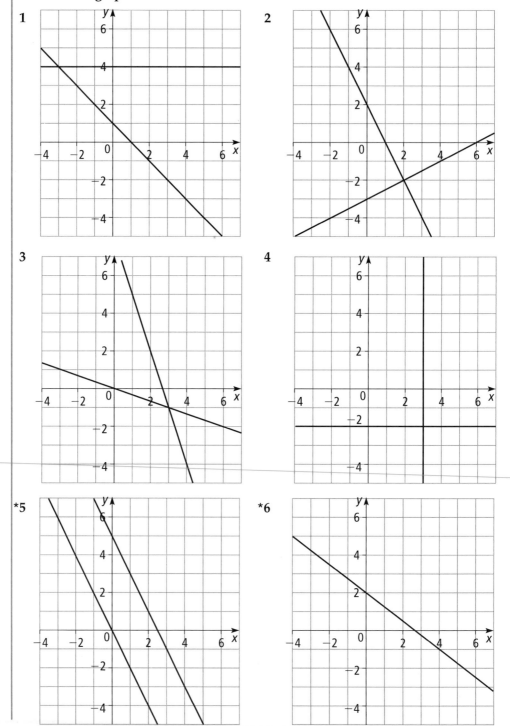

Simultaneous equations

A $y = -2$
   $x - 3 = 0$

B $y - \frac{1}{2}x = -3$
   $y + 2x = 2$

C $y = -2x + 5$
   $y + 2x = 0$

D $y + \frac{3}{4}x - 2 = 0$
   $4y = -3x + 8$

E $y + x = 1$
   $y - 4 = 0$

F $y = -3x + 8$
   $y + \frac{1}{3}x = 0$

Solutions

No solution

Infinite number of solutions

$x = 2, y = -2$

$x = 3, y = -2$

$x = 3, y = -1$

$x = -3, y = 4$

13

Shape, space and measures 6

The sine and cosine ratios

Leonhard Euler (1707–1783) lived in St Petersburg in Russia, and then in Berlin in Germany. He worked extensively in trigonometry and on inscribed and circumscribed circles. He was the first to use capital letters for the angles of a triangle and lower case letters for the sides. He also found a connection between the numbers of faces, edges and vertices (corners) of solids.

In Chapter 9, we used the tangent ratio in a right-angled triangle.

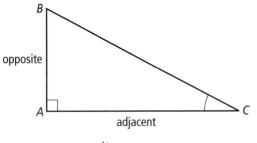

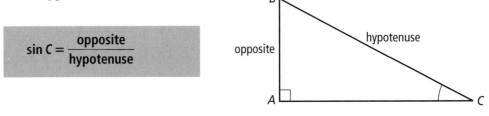

Remember that the sides named opposite and adjacent depend on the angle chosen in the triangle.

$$\tan C = \frac{\text{opposite}}{\text{adjacent}}$$

There are two other ratios used to calculate the lengths of sides, or sizes of angles, of right-angled triangles.

The sine ratio

The ratio of the length of the side opposite a chosen angle divided by the length of the hypotenuse is the **sine ratio**.

$$\sin C = \frac{\text{opposite}}{\text{hypotenuse}}$$

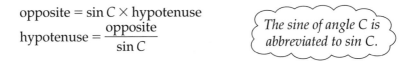

We can rearrange this formula to give two other forms:

$$\text{opposite} = \sin C \times \text{hypotenuse}$$
$$\text{hypotenuse} = \frac{\text{opposite}}{\sin C}$$

The sine of angle C is abbreviated to sin C.

Worked example

Calculate the size of angle x in this diagram.

$$\sin x = \frac{\text{opposite}}{\text{hypotenuse}}$$

$$= \frac{6}{14}$$

$$= 0.428$$

Angle $x = \sin^{-1} 0.428 = 25.4° \text{ (1 dp)}.$

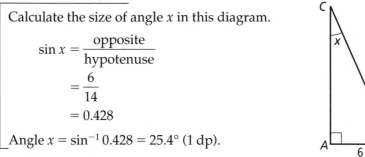

EXERCISE 13.1

Use the sine ratio to calculate the size of the angle marked x in each of these diagrams.

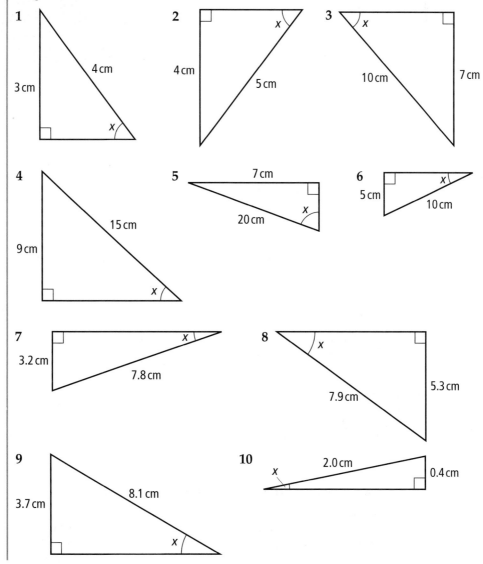

1 4 cm, 3 cm, x

2 4 cm, 5 cm, x

3 x, 10 cm, 7 cm

4 15 cm, 9 cm, x

5 7 cm, 20 cm, x

6 5 cm, x, 10 cm

7 3.2 cm, x, 7.8 cm

8 x, 7.9 cm, 5.3 cm

9 3.7 cm, 8.1 cm, x

10 x, 2.0 cm, 0.4 cm

Worked examples

(i) Use the sine ratio to calculate the length of side AB in this diagram.

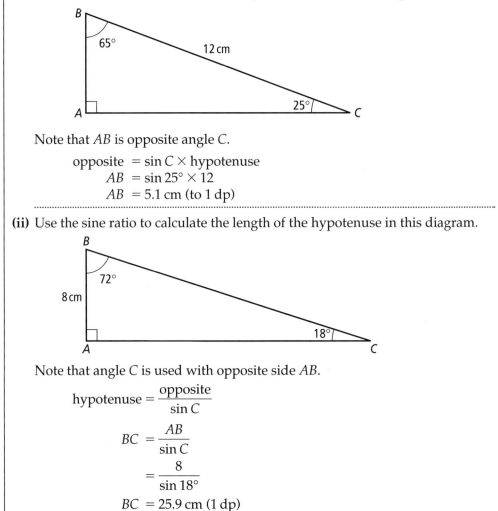

Note that AB is opposite angle C.

$$\text{opposite} = \sin C \times \text{hypotenuse}$$
$$AB = \sin 25° \times 12$$
$$AB = 5.1 \text{ cm (to 1 dp)}$$

(ii) Use the sine ratio to calculate the length of the hypotenuse in this diagram.

Note that angle C is used with opposite side AB.

$$\text{hypotenuse} = \frac{\text{opposite}}{\sin C}$$

$$BC = \frac{AB}{\sin C}$$

$$= \frac{8}{\sin 18°}$$

$$BC = 25.9 \text{ cm (1 dp)}$$

EXERCISE 13.2

Use the sine ratio to calculate the length of the side AB in each of these diagrams.

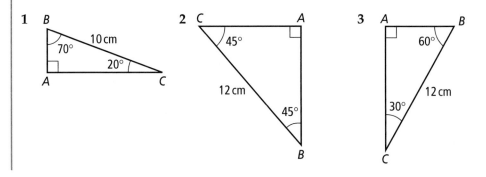

1

2

3

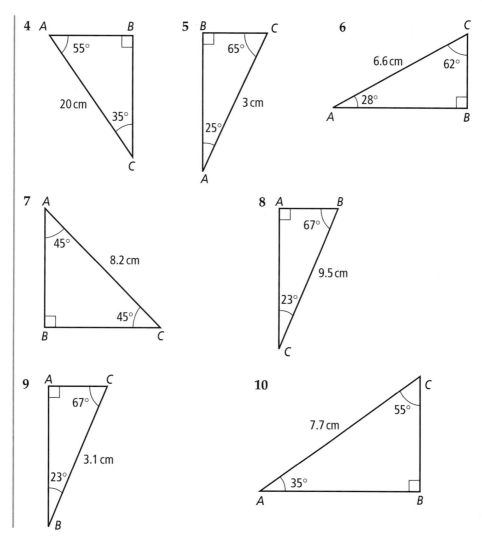

Use the sine ratio to calculate the length of the hypotenuse of each of these right-angled triangles.

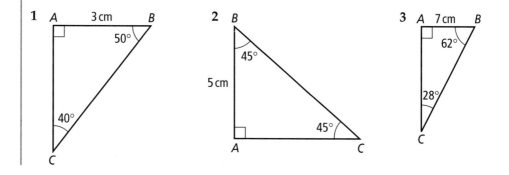

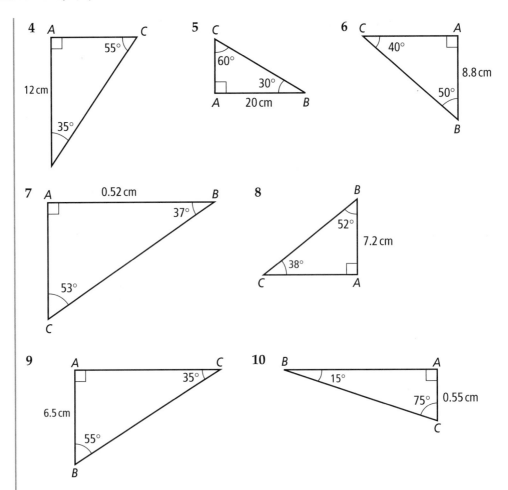

The cosine ratio

The ratio of the length of the side adjacent to a chosen angle divided by the length of the hypotenuse is the **cosine ratio**.

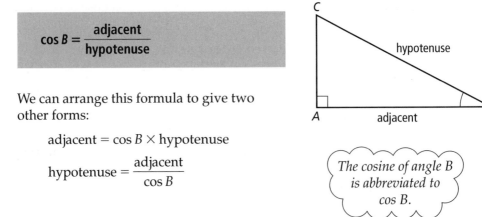

$$\cos B = \frac{\text{adjacent}}{\text{hypotenuse}}$$

We can arrange this formula to give two other forms:

$$\text{adjacent} = \cos B \times \text{hypotenuse}$$

$$\text{hypotenuse} = \frac{\text{adjacent}}{\cos B}$$

The cosine of angle B is abbreviated to cos B.

Worked examples

(i) Calculate the size of angle B is this diagram.

$$\cos B = \frac{\text{adjacent}}{\text{hypotenuse}}$$

$$= \frac{6}{14}$$

$$= 0.429$$

Angle $B = \cos^{-1} 0.429$
$= 64.6°$ (1 dp)

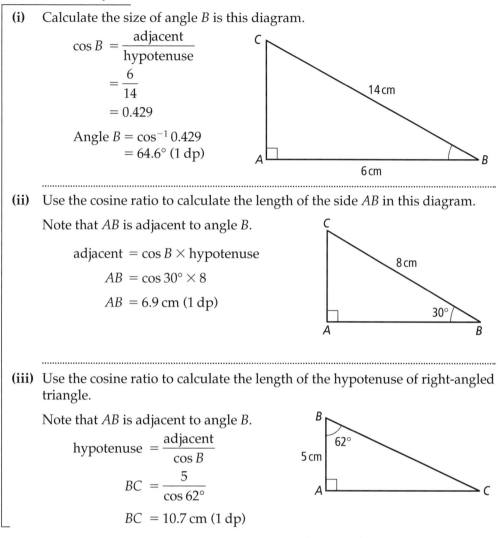

(ii) Use the cosine ratio to calculate the length of the side AB in this diagram.

Note that AB is adjacent to angle B.

$$\text{adjacent} = \cos B \times \text{hypotenuse}$$

$$AB = \cos 30° \times 8$$

$$AB = 6.9 \text{ cm (1 dp)}$$

(iii) Use the cosine ratio to calculate the length of the hypotenuse of right-angled triangle.

Note that AB is adjacent to angle B.

$$\text{hypotenuse} = \frac{\text{adjacent}}{\cos B}$$

$$BC = \frac{5}{\cos 62°}$$

$$BC = 10.7 \text{ cm (1 dp)}$$

EXERCISE 13.4

Use the cosine ratio to calculate the size of the angle marked x in each of these diagrams.

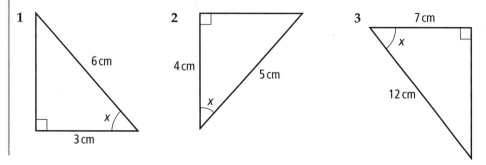

1 6 cm 3 cm x

2 4 cm 5 cm x

3 7 cm x 12 cm

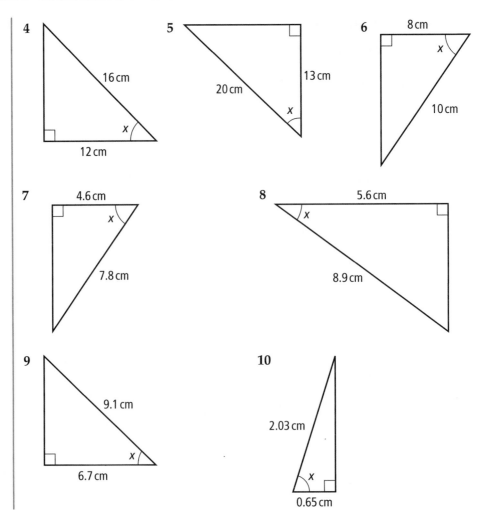

4   16 cm   12 cm   x

5   20 cm   13 cm   x

6   8 cm   x   10 cm

7   4.6 cm   x   7.8 cm

8   5.6 cm   x   8.9 cm

9   9.1 cm   x   6.7 cm

10   2.03 cm   x   0.65 cm

EXERCISE 13.5

Use the cosine ratio to calculate the length of the side *AB* in each of these diagrams.

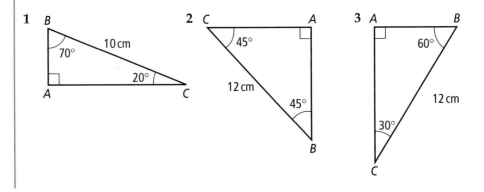

1 B   10 cm   70°   20°   A   C

2 C   45°   12 cm   45°   A   B

3 A   60°   12 cm   30°   B   C

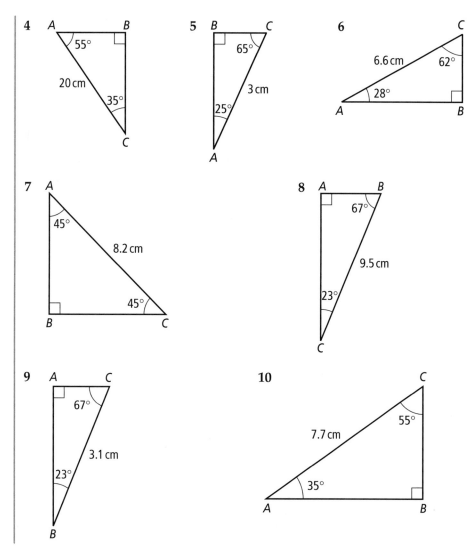

4 Triangle ABC: angle A = 55°, angle B = 90°, AC = 20 cm, angle C = 35°

5 Triangle with angle B = 90°, angle C = 65°, BC = 3 cm, angle A = 25°

6 6.6 cm, angle C = 62°, angle A = 28°, angle B = 90°

7 angle A = 45°, AC = 8.2 cm, angle B = 90°, angle C = 45°

8 angle A = 90°, angle B = 67°, 9.5 cm, angle C = 23°

9 angle A = 90°, angle C = 67°, 3.1 cm, angle B = 23°

10 angle C = 55°, 7.7 cm, angle A = 35°, angle B = 90°

EXERCISE 13.6

Use the cosine ratio to calculate the length of the hypotenuse in each of these diagrams.

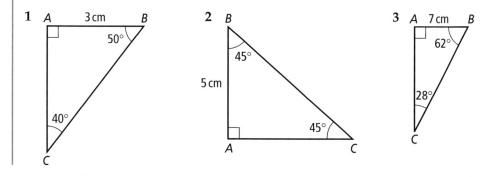

1 A 3 cm B, angle 50°, angle A = 90°, angle 40°, C

2 B, angle 45°, 5 cm, angle A = 90°, angle 45°, C

3 A 7 cm B, angle 62°, angle 28°, C

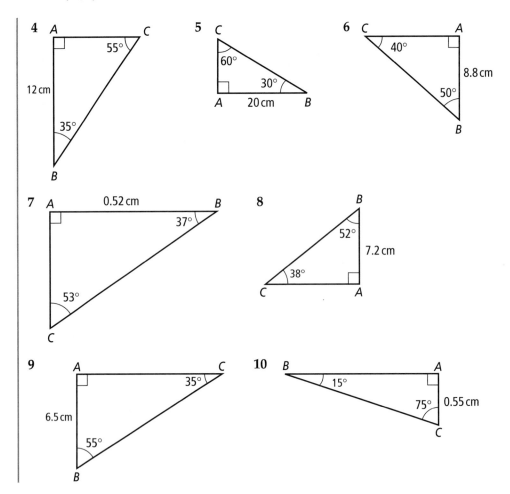

Did you notice that the diagrams in this exercise were the same as those in Exercise 13.3? The answer you got for the length of each hypotenuse should therefore have been the same. This shows a link between cosine and sine.

EXERCISE 13.7

Copy and complete this table.

Angle x	sin x	Angle (90° − x)	cos (90° − x)
5°		85°	
10°		80°	
15°			
20°			
25°			
30°			
35°			
40°			
45°			

You should notice from your completed table that:

$$\sin x = \cos (90° - x)$$

Similarly:

$$\cos x = \sin (90° - x)$$

> *In any right-angled triangle, the two angles that are not right angles must add up to 90° since all three angles total 180°.*

When solving problems involving right-angled triangles, you often have a choice of methods you can use (cos, sin or tan ratios, or Pythagoras' rule). The choice depends on what information you have, and what you want to find.

EXERCISE 13.8

Use trigonometry (tan, cos or sin) and/or Pythagoras' rule to find the lengths of the unknown sides (in cm), and the sizes of the unknown angles (in degrees) in these triangles.

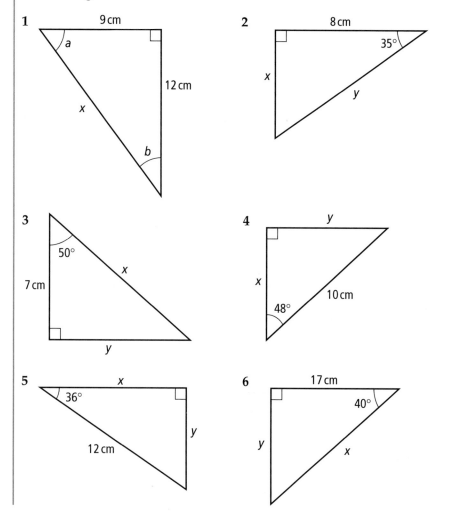

7

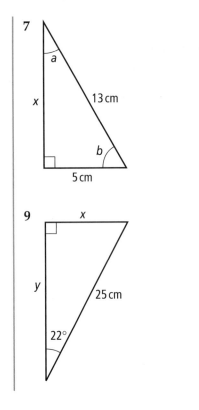

a

x   13 cm

b

5 cm

8

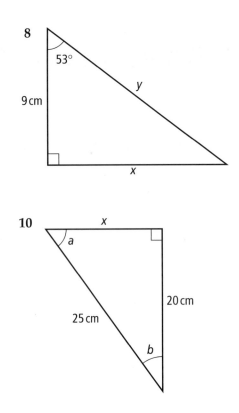

53°

y

9 cm

x

9   *x*

y

25 cm

22°

10   *x*

a

20 cm

25 cm

b

14

Shape, space and measures 7

Simple loci

A **locus** (plural **loci**) describes where a series of points lie, when the points fit a particular rule.

The points can create a region, a line or both.

Most simple problems involving loci involve one of these types:

- points at a fixed distance from a point
- points at a fixed distance from a straight line
- points at the same distance from two points.

The locus of points at a fixed distance from a given point

Worked example

Imagine a point labelled O. What is the locus of all points 5 cm from O?

The diagram below shows four points, each 5 cm from O.

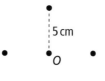

However, these are not the only points which can be plotted 5 cm from O. This diagram shows more points plotted 5 cm from O.

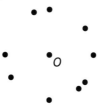

Once again, however, these are not the only points. In fact if you draw a circle with its centre at O and with a radius of 5 cm, then every point on the circumference of the circle is 5 cm from O.

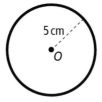

The locus of all the points 5 cm from O is therefore the circumference of this circle.

The locus of points at a given distance from a given straight line

Worked example

Imagine a straight line *AB*. What is the locus of all the points 5 cm from *AB*?

The diagram below shows four points, all 5 cm from the line *AB*. Note that these distances are measured at right angles to the line.

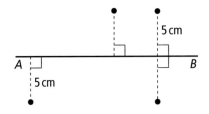

However, more points can be plotted 5 cm from *AB*, as shown in this diagram.

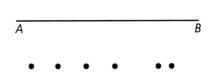

In fact, if you draw two lines through the points on either side of *AB*, parallel to *AB*, then every point on the lines will be 5 cm from *AB*.

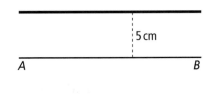

The parallel lines either side of *AB* are therefore the locus of all the points 5 cm from *AB*.

However, the diagram does not include the points at the two ends of the line *AB*. If these two points are taken into account, then the locus becomes more complicated, as shown.

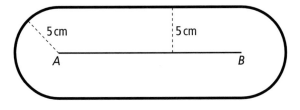

As ends of the line *AB* are points, the locus of the points 5 cm from each of them must be part of a circle.

The locus of points equidistant from two given points

Worked example

Two points M and N are shown. What is the locus of all the points that are equidistant (the same distance) from points M and N?

$M \bullet$

$N \bullet$

This diagram shows four points, all equidistant from M and N.

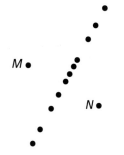

Once again, there are other points which are equidistant from M and N.

All the points that are equidistant from M and N in fact lie on the perpendicular bisector of MN.

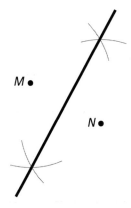

Therefore the perpendicular bisector of MN is the locus of all the points that are equidistant from points M and N.

EXERCISE 14.1

You will need a pair of compasses and a ruler for this exercise.

1   Draw the locus of all the points that are 6 cm from a point X.

2   The points X and Y are 8 cm apart.

$X \bullet\text{-------------------}\bullet Y$
        8 cm

   Draw a scale drawing of the diagram and draw the locus of points that are equidistant from both points X and Y.

3   Draw a line CD 10 cm long. Draw the locus of all the points 4 cm from the line, including its end points.

4   Two points X and Y are 7 cm apart as shown.

$X \bullet\text{----}$
               7 cm
                    $\text{----}\bullet Y$

   (a) Copy the diagram and draw the locus of all the points equidistant from X and Y.
   (b) A third point Z is 6 cm below X. Find the locus of points equidistant from points X, Y and Z.

5   Two points L and M are 6 cm apart. Find the locus of points 4 cm from both L and M.

So far we have only looked at cases where the locus is a line (straight or curved). The locus can, however, also be a region or area.

Worked examples

(i) A garden is 10 m × 10 m. In its centre is an apple tree. Grass cannot be planted within 2 m of the tree.
   (a) Draw a scale drawing of the garden.
   (b) Shade the locus of points where the grass can be planted.

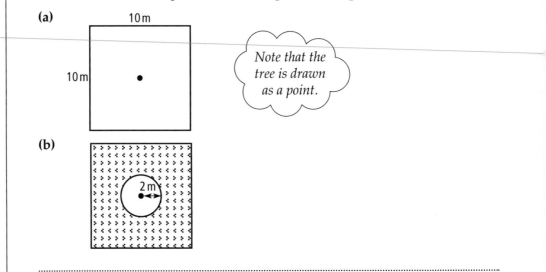

Note that the tree is drawn as a point.

(ii) A garden is 10 m × 15 m. Grass can only be planted where it is further than
4 m from each of the four corners of the garden.
(a) Draw a scale drawing of the garden.
(b) Shade the locus of points where the grass can be planted.

(a)

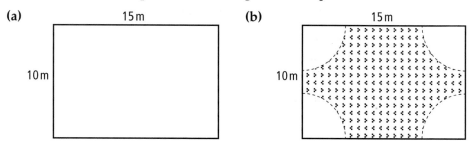

Notice that this time the boundaries are drawn as a dashed line. This is
because they are not included in the locus of points, as the grass can only be
planted at a distance greater than 4 m from each corner.

If the boundary *is* included in the locus of points (as in example **(i)**), it is
drawn as a solid line. If the boundary is *not* included in the locus of points (as
in example **(ii)**), it is drawn as a dashed line.

EXERCISE 14.2

1   A goat is tied to a rail 8 m long. The rope tying the goat to the rail is 3 m in
length and is free to slide along the whole length of the rail.

(a) Draw a scale diagram of the rail.
(b) Construct the locus of all the points that can be reached by the goat.

2   The diagram shows a plan view of a rectangular garden 10 m × 8 m in size.
The wall of the house runs along one side of the garden.

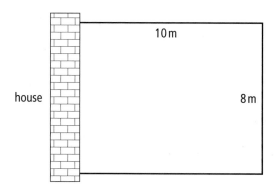

The owner of the house wants to grass the garden. However, the grass must be *more* than 4 m from the side of the house and *at least* 2 m from the edge of the rest of the garden.

(a) Draw a scale drawing of the garden.

(b) Draw the locus of all the points where the grass can be grown.

3 Two radio transmitters, Amber Radio and Beacon Radio, are 50 km apart. Beacon Radio is south-east of Amber Radio.

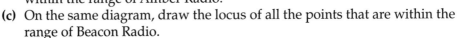

Amber Radio has a range of 40 km; Beacon Radio has a range of 30 km.

(a) Draw a scale diagram of the position of the two radio transmitters.

(b) Draw the locus of all the points that are within the range of Amber Radio.

(c) On the same diagram, draw the locus of all the points that are within the range of Beacon Radio.

(d) Shade on your diagram the region that falls within the range of both radio transmitters.

4 Three water sprinklers (*X*, *Y* and *Z*) are placed in a field. Their positions relative to each other are shown in the diagram.

Sprinklers *X* and *Y* have a maximum range of 10 m; *Z* has a maximum range of 15 m.

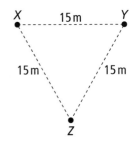

(a) Draw a scale diagram of the position of the sprinklers.

(b) Construct the locus of all the points that can be reached by each of the three sprinklers.

(c) Shade the region that can be reached by all three sprinklers.

5 This garden is in the shape of a trapezium.

A garden designer wishes to build a flower bed in the garden. The flower bed must be further than 3 m from the edge of the garden.

(a) Draw a scale drawing of the garden.

(b) Construct the locus of all the points where the flower bed can be built.

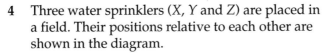

6 This diagram is a plan view of a girl standing on one side of a brick wall. The wall is taller than the girl, so she cannot see over it.

(a) Copy the diagram.

(b) On your diagram identify the locus of points that the girl cannot see.

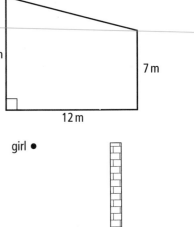

7   Three children, Alex, James and Sofia, are standing near a wall. Alex and James are on one side of the wall, Sofia on the other. None of them is able to see over the wall.

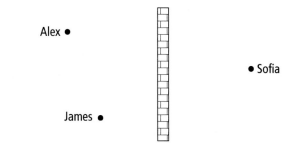

(a) Draw a copy of the diagram.
(b) Identify the locus of points where Sofia should stand if she wants to remain hidden from Alex and James.
(c) Identify the locus of points where Sofia should stand if she wants to remain hidden from James but visible to Alex.
(d) Identify the locus of points where Sofia should stand if she wants to remain hidden from Alex but visible to James.

8   A cage is in the shape of a quadrant. The perpendicular sides have a length of 6 m. A path needs to be built around the cage. It must have a constant width of 2 m.

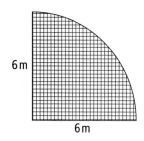

(a) Draw a scale drawing of the cage.
(b) Construct the locus of all the points occupied by the path.

15

Using and applying mathematics/ICT 3

ICT activity

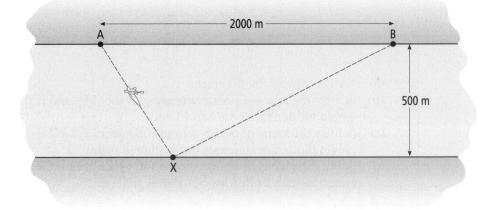

The little village of Watermead has an annual rowing race. Contestants have to row from point A on one side of the river to the opposite bank and then back to point B on the same bank as A. The rules state that a rower can turn at any point on the opposite bank – that is, point X can be anywhere along the opposite river bank.

1 Using Cabri or a similar geometry package, work out the shortest possible distance that a rower can row.

   Set up your screen similar to this one.

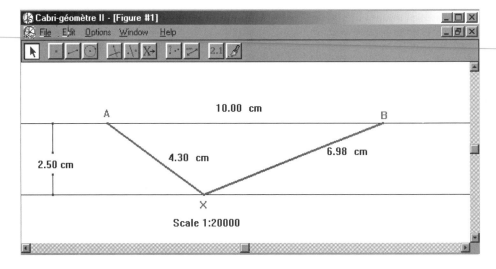

2   Use a spreadsheet to model the problem and find the shortest distance
$AX + XB$ correct to 2 dp.

A simplified diagram of the information is:

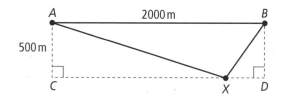

Set up your spreadsheet in a similar way to this:

	A	B	C	D	E	F
	Distance AC	Distance CX	Distance XD	Distance AX	Distance XB	Total
1	(m)	(m)	(m)	(m)	(m)	Distance (m)
2	500					
3	500					
4	500					
5	500					
6	500					
7						
8			Enter formulae here		Enter formulae using	
9					Pythagoras here	

Investigation

In the ICT activity you found the shortest possible value for $AX + XB$ and
therefore the shortest distance that the rower needs to row.

By using either the sine or the cosine ratio and using your solutions from the ICT
activity, advise a rower as to the direction he/she should set off at, that is,

(a) calculate the optimum size for angle a
(b) calculate the optimum size for angle b.

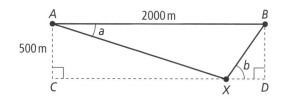

Summary

At the end of this section you should know:
- how to calculate the upper and lower bounds of a number
- how to write the upper and lower bounds of a number as an inequality
- how to represent the upper and lower bounds on a number line
- how to plot lines represented by simultaneous equations of the form $y = mx + c$ and find their solution
- ⋆ how to plot lines represented by simultaneous equations *not* given in the form $y = mx + c$ and find their solution
- ⋆ that some simultaneous equations produce no solutions
- ⋆ that some simultaneous equations produce an infinite number of solutions
- how to use the sine ratio to find the length of the opposite side or the hypotenuse or the size of an angle in a right-angled triangle
- how to use the cosine ratio to find the length of the adjacent side or the hypotenuse or the size of an angle in a right-angled triangle
- how to find the locus of points that are a given distance from a fixed point
- how to find the locus of points that are a given distance from a straight line
- how to find the locus of points that equidistant from two fixed points
- how to find a locus of points that is a region or area rather than a line
- the different ways of representing loci when the boundary is/isn't included in the description.

Review 3A

1 Each of these numbers is shown to the nearest whole number.
   (a) 20   **(b)** 100

   For each number:
   (i) give the upper and lower bounds
   (ii) using x to represent the number, write the range of its values as an inequality.

2 Each of these numbers is correct to the number of decimal places shown in brackets.
   (a) 15.2 (1 dp)   **(b)** 0.88 (2 dp)

   For each number:
   (i) give the upper and lower bounds
   (ii) using x to represent the number, write the range of its values as an inequality.

3 (a) Plot the lines represented by these equations on the same co-ordinate grid.

$$y = 3x - 4 \quad \text{and} \quad y = -\tfrac{1}{2}x + 3$$

   (b) Use your graph to find the solution to the simultaneous equations:

$$y = 3x - 4$$
$$y = -\tfrac{1}{2}x + 3$$

* 4 Solve these simultaneous equations graphically.

$$x - y = 3$$
$$2x + y = 6$$

* 5 Explain, giving reasons, whether each of these pairs of simultaneous equations has one solution, no solution or an infinite number of solutions.
   (a) $y = x + 1$ **(b)** $y = 3x - 2$
         $y = -x + 1$ $y = 3x + 2$

6 Calculate the size of angle a in this right-angled triangle. Give your answer to the nearest whole number.

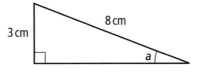

* 7 Using trigonometry, explain whether the triangle ABC is right angled.

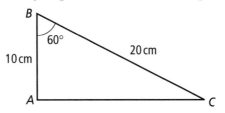

8 Using trigonometry, calculate the lengths of the sides marked p and q (in cm to 1 dp).

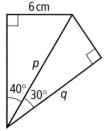

9 Two points X and Y are 8 cm apart as shown.

(a) Copy the diagram to scale.

(b) Construct the locus of all the points that are equidistant from both X and Y.

10 A courtyard is in the shape of a right-angled triangle with dimensions as shown.

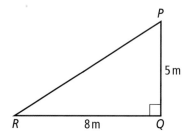

The owner of the courtyard wishes to place some flower pots in the courtyard. However, the pots must be at least 3 m from each of the three corners of the courtyard.

(a) Draw a scale drawing of the courtyard.

(b) Shade the locus of all the points where the pots could be placed.

Review 3B

1 Each of these numbers is shown to the nearest whole number.
(a) 5 **(b)** 0

For each number:
(i) give the upper and lower bounds
(ii) represent the range of values on a number line.

2 Each of these numbers is correct to the number of decimal places shown in brackets.
(a) 10.0 (1 dp) **(b)** 10.00 (2 dp)

For each number:
(i) give the upper and lower bounds
(ii) represent the range of values on a number line.

3 (a) Plot the lines represented by these equations on the same co-ordinate grid.

$$y = -1 \quad \text{and} \quad y = -2x + 3$$

(b) Use your graph to find the solution to the two simultaneous equations:

$$y = -1$$
$$y = -2x + 3$$

*4 Solve these simultaneous equations graphically.

$$y + x = 4$$
$$3y + x = 6$$

*5 Explain, giving reasons, whether each of these pairs of simultaneous equations has one solution, no solution or an infinite number of solutions.

(a) $y = 2x - 1$ **(b)** $x = 4$
    $3y = 6x - 3$ $x = 0$

6 Calculate the size of angle b in this right-angled triangle. Give your answer to the nearest whole number.

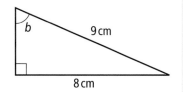

*7 Using trigonometry, explain whether the angle XYZ is a right angle.

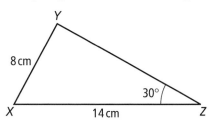

8 (a) Using trigonometry, calculate the length of the sides marked a and b (in cm to 1 dp).

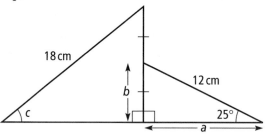

(b) Calculate the size of angle c, giving your answer to two significant figures.

9 Three points P, Q and R are spaced as shown.

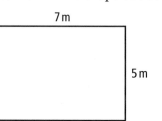

Copy the diagram and find, by construction, the locus of points equidistant from P, Q and R.

10 The plan of a classroom in the shape of a rectangle is shown.

7 m

5 m

The teacher wants to arrange the pupils' desks in such a way that they are all more than 1 m from the edges of the room.
(a) Draw a scale drawing of the classroom.
(b) Shade the locus of all the points where the desks could be placed.

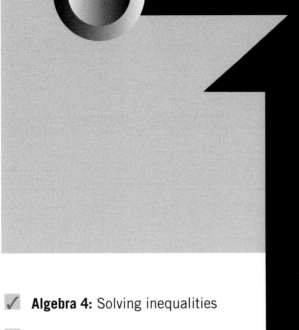

SECTION FOUR

16

Algebra 4

Solving inequalities

In Book 2, and in Chapter 11 of this book, you learned about the meaning of an inequality and how it can be represented on a number line. For example, $x \geqslant 3$ means that the value of x is greater than or equal to 3. It can be shown on a number line like this:

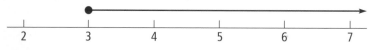

More complex inequalities such as $x - 2 > 4$ need to be **solved** to give $x > 6$. To solve inequalities you can use a similar method to the one you use to solve equations: whatever you do to one side of the inequality, you must also do to the other.

Worked example

Solve these inequalities and represent the solutions on a number line.
(a) $3x - 2 > x + 2$ **(b)** $4x + 1 \geqslant 5x - 3$

(a) $3x - 2 > x + 2$
$$2x - 2 > 2 \qquad \text{(subtract } x \text{ from both sides)}$$
$$2x > 4 \qquad \text{(add 2 to both sides)}$$
$$x > 2 \qquad \text{(divide both sides by 2)}$$

(b) $4x + 1 \geqslant 5x - 3$
$$1 \geqslant x - 3 \qquad \text{(subtract } 4x \text{ from both sides)}$$
$$4 \geqslant x \qquad \text{(add 3 to both sides)}$$
$$x \leqslant 4 \qquad \text{(turn the inequality round)}$$

EXERCISE 16.1

Solve these inequalities.
1 **(a)** $x - 3 \leqslant 4$ **(b)** $x + 2 > 1$
2 **(a)** $2x + 4 \geqslant 0$ **(b)** $3x + 1 < 4$
3 **(a)** $3x - 2 \leqslant 2x$ **(b)** $6x + 4 \geqslant 5x$
4 **(a)** $5x + 6 > 3x + 8$ **(b)** $7x - 3 < 4x + 3$
5 **(a)** $3x - 4 < 5x + 2$ **(b)** $5x + 1 \leqslant 9x - 5$
6 **(a)** $x + 8 \geqslant 5x - 1$ **(b)** $2x \leqslant 5x$

Multiplication or division by a negative number

So far we have solved inequalities in the same way as we solve equations.

Usually, when you use the same operation on both sides, the inequality stays true.

$5 > 3$ 5 is greater than 3, a true statement

Adding 3 to both sides gives:

$8 > 6$ 8 is greater than 6, still a true statement

Subtracting 4 from both sides gives:

$4 > 2$ 4 is greater than 2, still a true statement

Multiplying both sides of 6 gives:

$24 > 12$ 24 is greater than 12, still a true statement

Dividing both sides by 3 gives:

$8 > 4$ 8 is greater than 4, still a true statement

So far, when the same thing is done to both sides of the inequality, the inequality remains true. In this respect it behaves like an equation. However, the examples below show that this is not always the case.

$4 > 3$ 4 is greater than 3, a true statement

Multiplying both sides by -2 gives:

$-8 > -6$ -8 is greater than -6, a **false** statement

To make this statement correct, the inequality sign needs to be reversed, that is:

$-8 < -6$ -8 is less than -6, now a true statement

A similar problem occurs when dividing by a negative number.

$10 > 8$ 10 is greater than 8, a true statement

Dividing both sides by -2 gives:

$-5 > -4$ -5 is greater than -4, a **false** statement

If the inequality sign is reversed, it then becomes correct:

$-5 < -4$ -5 is less than -4, now a true statement

Therefore inequalities can be solved in the same way as solving equations *except* when both sides are either multiplied or divided by a negative number. In this case, the inequality sign must be reversed to keep the statement true.

Worked example

Solve this inequality: $-3x - 4 > 2$.

$$-3x - 4 > 2$$
$$-3x > 6 \qquad \text{(add 4 to both sides)}$$
$$x < -2 \qquad \text{(divide both sides by } -3\text{)}$$

Note that the inequality sign has changed direction.

EXERCISE 16.2

Solve these inequalities.

1 (a) $-2x + 6 < 8$ (b) $-x - 4 \geqslant 5$

2 (a) $3 - 4x > 11$ (b) $5 - x \geqslant 0$

3 (a) $-\frac{1}{2}x + 2 \leqslant 3$ (b) $-2 - \frac{1}{2}x > 5$

4 (a) $4 - \frac{1}{3}x \leqslant 0$ (b) $1 - \frac{2}{5}x \leqslant -1$

5 (a) $2(3 - x) > -4$ (b) $\frac{1}{2}(4 - x) > 2$

6 (a) $\dfrac{x + 1}{2} > -1$ (b) $\dfrac{1 - x}{3} \leqslant -1$

7 (a) $\dfrac{1 - 2x}{4} \geqslant -2$ (b) $\dfrac{-3x}{2} < -6$

8 (a) $\dfrac{4 - \frac{1}{2}x}{3} < 7$ (b) $\dfrac{-2 - \frac{1}{3}x}{5} \leqslant 2$

Solving combined inequalities

You also saw in Book 2, and in Chapter 11 of this book, that some inequalities could be described with two inequality signs, for example $3 \leqslant x < 7$. You show this on a number line like this:

An inequality with two inequality signs can still be solved in the same way as before, if it is broken down into two separate inequalities. For example, to solve

$$6 \leqslant 2x - 2 < 15$$

first split it into two:

$$6 \leqslant 2x - 2 \quad \text{and} \quad 2x - 2 < 15$$

Solve each inequality separately:

$$
\begin{aligned}
6 &\leqslant 2x - 2 \\
8 &\leqslant 2x \qquad \text{(add 2 to both sides)} \\
4 &\leqslant x \qquad \text{(divide both sides by 2)} \\
x &\geqslant 4
\end{aligned}
$$

$$
\begin{aligned}
2x - 2 &< 15 \\
2x &< 17 \qquad \text{(add 2 to both sides)} \\
x &< 8\tfrac{1}{2} \qquad \text{(divide both sides by 2)}
\end{aligned}
$$

These solutions can be represented on the following number line:

EXERCISE 16.3

Solve these inequalities. Represent each solution on a number line.

1 $3 < x + 2 \leqslant 6$

2 $5 \leqslant 3x - 1 \leqslant 11$

3 $8 < 2(x - 4) \leqslant 10$

4 $12 \leqslant 3(1 - x) < 21$

5 $1 \geqslant x \geqslant 2$

6 $6 \geqslant 2(x + 1) > 12$

7 $12 \geqslant 3(2x - 1) \geqslant 33$

8 $-2 + x < -x \leqslant 4x - 10$

Solving quadratic equations using factors

Abu Ja'far Muhammad Ibn Musa Al-Khwarizmi is called 'the father of algebra'. He was born in Baghdad in AD 790 and wrote the book *Hisab al-jabr w'al-muqabala* in 830, from which the word algebra (*al-jabr*) is taken. He found solutions to quadratic equations and also wrote about Hindu-Arabic numbers.

An expression such as $x^2 + 5x + 6$ is known as a **quadratic expression** because the highest power of any of its terms is 'squared' – in this case x^2. It can be **factorised** by writing it as a product of two brackets.

Worked examples

(i) Factorise $x^2 + 5x + 6$.

Set up a 2×2 multiplication grid to help you find the factors.

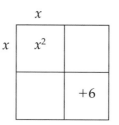

As there is only one term in x^2, this can be entered on the grid, as can the constant $+6$. The only two values which multiply to give x^2 are x and x. These too can be entered. We now need to find two values which multiply to give $+6$ and which add to give $+5$.

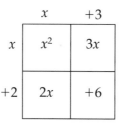

The only two values which satisfy both these conditions are $+3$ and $+2$. Therefore $x^2 + 5x + 6 = (x + 3)(x + 2)$.

(ii) Factorise $x^2 + 2x - 24$.

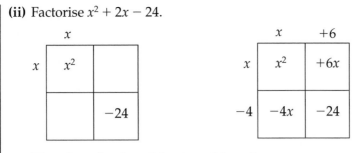

Therefore $x^2 + 2x - 24 = (x + 6)(x - 4)$

EXERCISE 17.1

Factorise these quadratic expressions.

1   $a^2 + 6a + 8$ 2 $b^2 + 7b + 12$
3   $c^2 + 8c + 15$ 4 $d^2 + 11d + 24$
5   $e^2 + 4e + 3$ 6 $f^2 + 11f + 18$
7   $g^2 + 18g + 77$ 8 $h^2 + 6h + 9$
9   $j^2 + 20j + 100$ 10 $k^2 + 8k + 16$

EXERCISE 17.2

Factorise these quadratic expressions.

1   $a^2 - 5a + 6$ 2 $b^2 - 9b + 20$
3   $c^2 - 5c + 4$ 4 $d^2 - 17d + 72$
5   $e^2 - 12e + 35$ 6 $f^2 - 3f + 2$
7   $g^2 - 6g + 9$ 8 $h^2 - 14h + 49$
9   $j^2 - 22j + 121$ 10 $k^2 - 24k + 144$

EXERCISE 17.3

Factorise these quadratic expressions.

1   $a^2 + a - 6$ 2 $b^2 + 2b - 3$
3   $c^2 + 2c - 8$ 4 $d^2 + 2d - 63$
5   $e^2 + e - 30$ 6 $f^2 - f - 6$
7   $g^2 - g - 72$ 8 $h^2 - 2h - 3$
9   $j^2 - 4j - 12$ 10 $k^2 - 16$

EXERCISE 17.4

Factorise these quadratic expressions.

1   $a^2 + 6a + 9$ 2 $b^2 - 4b + 4$
3   $c^2 - 4$ 4 $d^2 - 16$
5   $e^2 + 2e - 15$ 6 $f^2 + 9f + 14$
7   $g^2 - 4g - 12$ 8 $h^2 - 81$
9   $j^2 - 10j + 25$ 10 $k^2 - 9$

A **quadratic equation** is an equation where the highest power is 'squared' (for example, x^2). Therefore $x^2 - 5x + 6 = 0$ is an example of a quadratic equation. When you are asked to solve a quadratic equation you have to find a value (or values) for x (or any other variable) that makes the left-hand side of the equation equal to the right-hand side. For example, to solve the equation $x^2 - 5x + 6 = 0$ you need to find a value (or values) of x which makes $x^2 - 5x + 6$ equal to zero.

One method of solving a quadratic equation is to factorise it.

Worked examples

(i) Solve this quadratic equation: $x^2 - 5x + 6 = 0$.

Factorising $x^2 - 5x + 6$ gives $(x - 3)(x - 2)$. So $x^2 - 5x + 6 = 0$ becomes

$$(x - 3)(x - 2) = 0$$

If two numbers multiplied together give zero, then at least one of them must be zero. For $(x - 3)(x - 2) = 0$, the two numbers are $(x - 3)$ and $(x - 2)$. Therefore:

either $(x - 3) = 0$ or $(x - 2) = 0$

$x = 3$ $x = 2$

You can check the solutions by substituting them into the left-hand side of the original equation.

Substituting $x = 3$ into $x^2 - 5x + 6 = 0$ gives:

$$3^2 - (5 \times 3) + 6 = 0$$
$$9 - 15 + 6 = 0$$
$$0 = 0 \checkmark$$

Substituting $x = 2$ into $x^2 - 5x + 6 = 0$ gives:

$$2^2 - (5 \times 2) + 6 = 0$$
$$4 - 10 + 6 = 0$$
$$0 = 0 \checkmark$$

Both solutions are correct.

(ii) Solve the quadratic equation $x^2 + 2x = 24$.

To factorise the quadratic equation, rearrange it so that all the terms are on the same side of the equation. The equation becomes:

$$x^2 + 2x - 24 = 0$$

Factorising gives:

$$(x + 6)(x - 4) = 0$$

So either $x + 6 = 0$ or $x - 4 = 0$

$x = -6$ or $x = 4$

Check the solutions work.

Substituting $x = -6$ into $x^2 + 2x - 24 = 0$ gives:

$$(-6)^2 + (2 \times -6) - 24 = 0$$
$$36 - 12 - 24 = 0$$
$$0 = 0 \checkmark$$

Substituting $x = 4$ into $x^2 + 2x - 24 = 0$ gives:

$$4^2 + (2 \times 4) - 24 = 0$$
$$16 + 8 - 24 = 0$$
$$0 = 0 \checkmark$$

EXERCISE 17.5

Solve these quadratic equation by factorisation.

1 $a^2 + 5a + 6 = 0$ 2 $b^2 + 7b + 12 = 0$

3 $c^2 + 17c + 72 = 0$ 4 $d^2 - d - 2 = 0$

5 $e^2 - 3e - 10 = 0$ 6 $f^2 - 3f - 18 = 0$

7 $g^2 - 5g = -6$ 8 $h^2 - 9h = -20$

9 $j^2 - 13j = -42$ 10 $k^2 + 6k + 9 = 0$

11 $l^2 + 8l + 16 = 0$ 12 $m^2 - 10m + 25 = 0$

13 $n^2 - 16n + 64 = 0$ 14 $p^2 - 2p + 1 = 0$

15 $q^2 + 2q = -1$ 16 $r^2 - 16r + 63 = 0$

17 $s^2 - 1 = 0$ 18 $t^2 - 9 = 0$

19 $v^2 = 25$ 20 $w^2 = 121$

Worked example

The area of the rectangle below is 12 cm². Calculate its length and width.

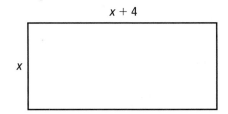

The area of the rectangle is given by the formula area = length × width. So

$$12 = x(x + 4)$$
$$= x^2 + 4x$$
$$x^2 + 4x - 12 = 0$$
$$(x + 6)(x - 2) = 0$$

so $x + 6 = 0$ therefore $x = -6$

or $x - 2 = 0$ therefore $x = +2$

$x = -6$ is not possible as the rectangle cannot have a negative length or width. So $x = 2$ is the solution. The measurements are therefore 2 cm and 6 cm.

EXERCISE 17.6

Given the area of each of these rectangles, find the length and width.

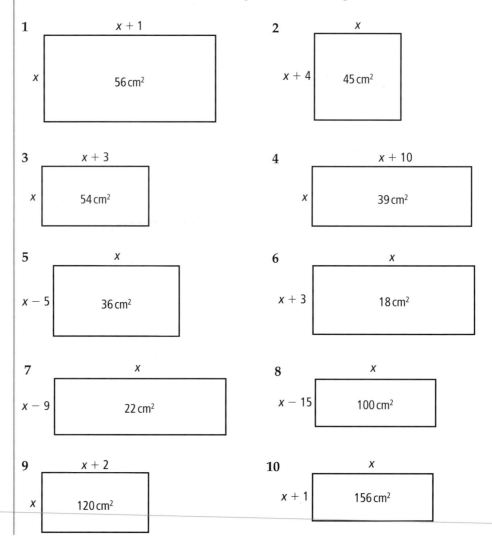

1 $x + 1$

x 56 cm²

2 x

$x + 4$ 45 cm²

3 $x + 3$

x 54 cm²

4 $x + 10$

x 39 cm²

5 x

$x - 5$ 36 cm²

6 x

$x + 3$ 18 cm²

7 x

$x - 9$ 22 cm²

8 x

$x - 15$ 100 cm²

9 $x + 2$

x 120 cm²

10 x

$x + 1$ 156 cm²

Volume of a sphere

In Book 2 you used formulae to calculate the volume of cuboids, cylinders and other prisms in general.
A sphere is not a prism but its volume can be calculated using the formula:

$$\text{volume} = \tfrac{4}{3}\pi r^3$$

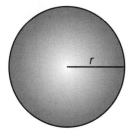

Worked examples

(i) Calculate the volume of this sphere.

$$\text{volume } = \tfrac{4}{3}\pi r^3$$

The radius = 3 cm.

$$\text{volume } = \tfrac{4}{3} \times \pi \times 3^3$$
$$= 113.1 \text{ cm}^3 \text{ (1 dp)}$$

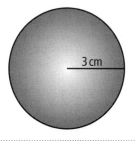

(ii) Calculate the volume of this sphere.

$$\text{volume } = \tfrac{4}{3}\pi r^3$$

The diameter = 10 cm, therefore the radius = 5 cm.

$$\text{volume } = \tfrac{4}{3} \times \pi \times 5^3$$
$$= 523.6 \text{ cm}^3$$

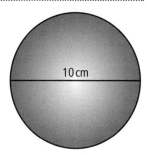

EXERCISE 18.1

Calculate the volume of each of the spheres in questions 1–4. Give your answers correct to 1 decimal place.

1

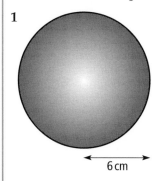

6 cm

2

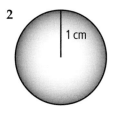

1 cm

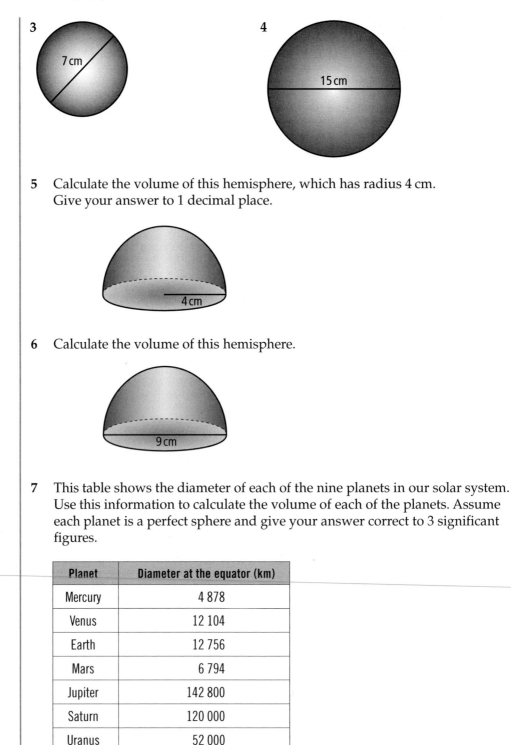

3   7 cm

4   15 cm

5   Calculate the volume of this hemisphere, which has radius 4 cm.
Give your answer to 1 decimal place.

4 cm

6   Calculate the volume of this hemisphere.

9 cm

7   This table shows the diameter of each of the nine planets in our solar system.
Use this information to calculate the volume of each of the planets. Assume
each planet is a perfect sphere and give your answer correct to 3 significant
figures.

Planet	Diameter at the equator (km)
Mercury	4 878
Venus	12 104
Earth	12 756
Mars	6 794
Jupiter	142 800
Saturn	120 000
Uranus	52 000
Neptune	48 400
Pluto	3 000

Worked example

A sphere has a volume of 2145 cm³. Calculate its radius to 1 decimal place.

Using the formula:

$$\text{volume} = \tfrac{4}{3}\pi r^3$$

$$2145 = \tfrac{4}{3}\pi r^3$$

$$r^3 = \frac{3 \times 2145}{4\pi} = 512$$

Therefore $r = \sqrt[3]{512}$

The radius of the sphere is 8.0 cm.

EXERCISE 18.2

For questions 1–6, the volumes of spheres are given. Calculate the radius of each sphere, giving your answer to 1 decimal place.

1   2500 cm³

2   1234 mm³

3   400 cm³

4   10 m³

5   1 000 000 cm³

6   1 cm³

7   Two balls A and B are shown below. The volume of ball A is 1000 cm³; ball B has a volume of 8000 cm³.

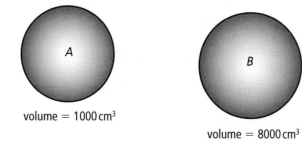

volume = 1000 cm³

volume = 8000 cm³

(a) Calculate to 1 decimal place the radius of ball A.
(b) Make a prediction for what you think will be the radius of ball B.
(c) Calculate to 1 decimal place the radius of ball B.
(d) Comment on your answer to part (c) compared with your prediction in part (b).

8 Two balls X and Y are shown below. The radius of ball X is 10 cm; the radius of ball Y is 20 cm.

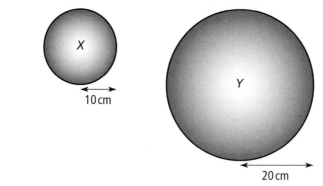

10 cm

20 cm

(a) Calculate the volume of ball X. Give your answer to 1 decimal place.
(b) Make a prediction for what you think will be the volume of ball Y.
(c) Calculate the volume of ball Y.
(d) Comment on your answer to part (c) compared with your prediction in part (b).

EXERCISE 18.3

1 A sphere just fits into a box that is the shape of a cube. The cube has an edge length of 6 cm.

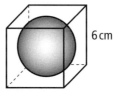

6 cm

(a) Calculate the volume of the cube.
(b) Calculate the volume of the sphere.
(c) What percentage of the space in the cube does the sphere occupy?

2 Two balls just fit into a cylindrical container of radius 4.5 cm.

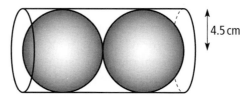

4.5 cm

(a) Calculate the volume of the cylinder.
(b) Calculate the volume occupied by both balls.
(c) What percentage of the space in the cylinder do the balls occupy?

3 A cube and a sphere have the same volume. If the cube has an edge length of 10 cm calculate (to 1 dp) the radius *r* (in cm) of the sphere.

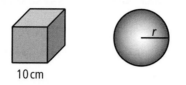

10 cm

4 An object is made from a cylinder with a hemisphere at each end.

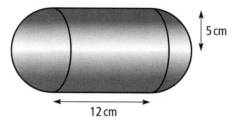

5 cm

12 cm

Calculate the volume of the object, giving your answer to the nearest whole number.

5 A metal bowl is made by taking a hemisphere and hollowing out another hemisphere from the inside. The thickness of the bowl is 3 mm and is constant throughout. The outer radius of the bowl is 8 cm.

8 cm   3 mm

Calculate, to 1 decimal place, the volume of metal needed to make the bowl.

6 This sphere and hemisphere have the same volume.

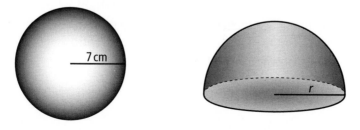

7 cm   *r*

If the radius of the sphere is 7 cm, calculate, to 1 decimal place, the radius *r* (in cm) of the hemisphere.

Shape, space and measures 9

Applications of Pythagoras and trigonometry

Earlier in this book you have studied the topics of Pythagoras's rule and trigonometry in their pure form. This chapter provides some practice in solving problems using Pythagoras's rule and trigonometry in a practical context.

Remember the three trigonometric formulae:

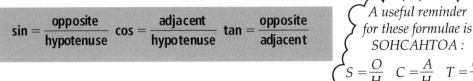

$$\sin = \frac{\text{opposite}}{\text{hypotenuse}} \quad \cos = \frac{\text{adjacent}}{\text{hypotenuse}} \quad \tan = \frac{\text{opposite}}{\text{adjacent}}$$

A useful reminder for these formulae is SOHCAHTOA :

$$S = \frac{O}{H} \quad C = \frac{A}{H} \quad T = \frac{O}{A}$$

Worked examples

(i) Calculate, using Pythagoras' rule, the length of the side marked x in this diagram.

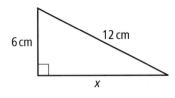

6 cm   12 cm

x

Pythagoras' rule states that $a^2 = b^2 + c^2$ where a is the length of the hypotenuse of a right-angled triangle and b and c are the lengths of the two shorter sides.

Substituting the given values into $a^2 = b^2 + c^2$ gives:

$$12^2 = 6^2 + x^2$$
$$144 = 36 + x^2$$
$$108 = x^2$$
$$x = \sqrt{108} = 10.4 \ (1 \text{ dp})$$

Therefore $x = 10.4$ cm

(ii) Using trigonometry, calculate the length of the side AB in this triangle.

By using SOHCAHTOA we can see that, to work out the length of AB, the tangent ratio must be used. Therefore:

$$\tan 50° = \frac{7}{AB}$$

$$AB = \frac{7}{\tan 50°} = 5.9 \ (1 \text{ dp})$$

Therefore $AB = 5.9$ cm.

C

7 cm

50°

A   B

(iii) Using trigonometry, calculate the size of the angle x in this diagram.

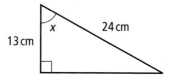

By using SOHCAHTOA we can see that, to calculate the size of x, the cosine ratio must be used. Therefore:

$$\cos x = \frac{13}{24} = 0.542 \text{ (3 dp)}$$

$$x = \cos^{-1} 0.542$$

Therefore $x = 57.2°$ (1 dp).

EXERCISE 19.1

1   An engineer marks out a rectangular plot of land $ABCD$.

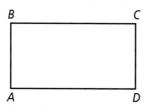

If $AB = 10$ m and $BC = 15$ m, using Pythagoras' rule, calculate the length AC, to 1 decimal place.

2   A ladder 4 m long is placed against the side of a house. The foot of the ladder must be at least 0.75 m from the house and no more than 1.2 m from it. Calculate:
(a) the maximum possible value of h
(b) the minimum possible value of h.

3   A communications mast is supported by ropes which are attached from the ground to a point half way up the mast. The communications mast is 60 m tall. If the distance from the base of the mast to the point where the rope is secured to the ground is 40 m, calculate the length of each of the support ropes.

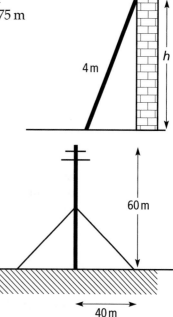

4   The horizontal distance between two hot-air balloons is 2.4 km. The difference in their vertical height is 300 m.

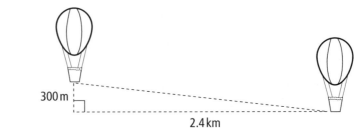

Calculate the direct distance between the two balloons.

5   Two planes are flying in formation. One plane is directly above the other. At a particular moment, their horizontal distance from a person standing at point X is 3.2 km. At the same moment, their true direct distances from X are 3.8 km and 3.7 km respectively.

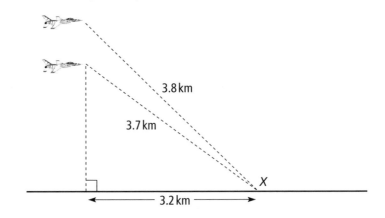

Calculate, in metres, the vertical height between the two planes.

6   Two boats set off at the same time from the same point. One heads north with a velocity of 10 km/h; the other heads due east with a velocity of 12 km/h.

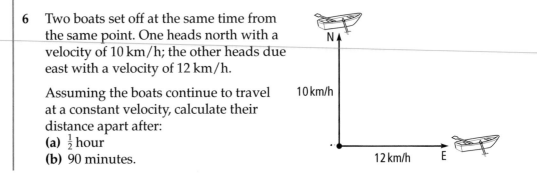

Assuming the boats continue to travel at a constant velocity, calculate their distance apart after:
(a) $\frac{1}{2}$ hour
(b) 90 minutes.

1   A person standing at point A is
20 m from the base of a tall tree. The
angle of the top of the tree from the
ground at point A is 35°.

Calculate the height of the tree to
the nearest centimetre.

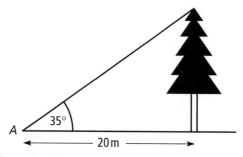

2   Two men are standing on the edges of two buildings at points P and Q. The
distance between the edges of the two buildings is 55 m. The angle of
elevation from P to Q is 8°. (The angle of elevation is the angle made with the
horizontal line of sight.)

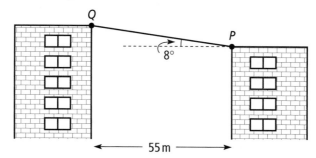

Calculate the difference in height between the two buildings. Give your
answer to 1 decimal place.

3   Two points on the ground, L and M, are 2 km apart. L is due north of M.
A person sets off from point M and heads due east with a velocity of 6 km/h.
After 1 hour he is at point X; after 2 hours he is at point Y.

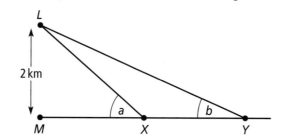

Calculate the size of the angles a and b.

4   The present height of the Pyramid of
Khafre in Egypt is 137 m. An engineer
surveying the pyramid measures an
angle of elevation of 33° from a point X
to the top of the pyramid. Calculate the
distance from X to the centre of the base
of the pyramid at Y.

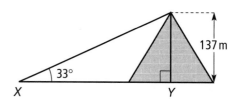

5 The tallest minaret in the world belongs to the Great Hassan II Mosque in Morocco.

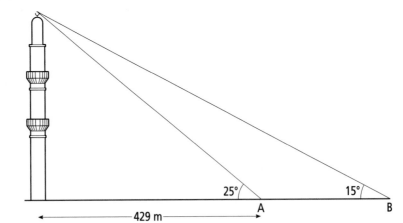

429 m

Two people standing in line with the minaret are looking up at it. One is at point A, the other at B. The angles of elevation from A and B to the top of the minaret are 25° and 15° respectively. If A is at a distance of 429 m from the centre of the minaret, calculate:

(a) the height of the minaret

(b) the distance between A and B.

6 A boat is moored 80 m from a cliff face. The angle of depression from the top of the cliff to the boat is 30°. The angle of depression from the top of the cliff to the anchor on the sea bed is 35°.

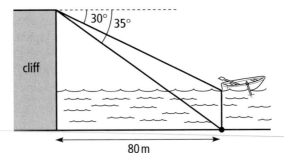

80 m

Calculate:

(a) the height of the cliff above sea level

(b) the depth of the sea directly below the boat.

7 Two cyclists set off at the same time from a point O. Cyclist P heads east with a velocity of 20 km/h. Cyclist Q heads north-west with a velocity of 16 km/h. After 45 minutes they both stop. Calculate:

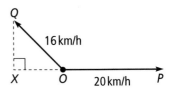

(a) the distance they have each travelled in 45 minutes

(b) the distance OX after 45 minutes

(c) the distance between P and Q when they both stop.

8 A ferris wheel, centre *O*, has a diameter of 10 m and carries eight equally spaced carriages for children to sit in. The carriages are numbered 1–8 as shown in the diagram. Calculate:

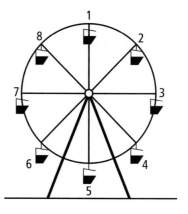

(a) the shortest distance between carriages 1 and 3

(b) the vertical height between carriages 2 and 4

(c) the shortest distance between carriages 1 and 4

(d) the angle of elevation from carriage 7 to carriage 2.

20 # Using and applying mathematics/ICT 4

Investigation

Different sports use different sized balls.

- How many times bigger is a football compared with a tennis ball?
- How many golf balls could fit in a basketball?

1 Collect a range of different sized spherical balls, such as tennis, football, basketball, volleyball, table-tennis, squash, etc.

2 Devise a way of measuring as accurately as possible the radius of each of the balls.

3 Use your results to calculate the volume of each of the balls.

4 Produce a graph (using a spreadsheet if possible) to compare the volumes of the different balls.

5 Answer the two questions posed at the start of this activity.

6 Pose some more questions of your own relating to the size of sports balls, and use your own data to answer them.

ICT activity

Investigate, using the internet as a resource, the history of Pythagoras's rule. Use your research to produce an information booklet for someone who has not yet studied Pythagoras.

Summary

At the end of this section you should know:
- how to solve inequalities
- how to represent the solution to inequalities on a number line
- how to factorise a quadratic expression
- how to solve quadratic equations by factorisation
- how to set up a quadratic equation from a given problem and solve it
- how to calculate the volume of a sphere
- * how to rearrange the formula for the volume of a sphere to make the radius the subject
- how to apply Pythagoras' rule to solve real problems
- how to apply the sine, cosine and tangent ratios to solve real problems
- how to identify which of the trigonometric ratios to use for a given problem.

Review 4A

1 Solve these inequalities.

(a) $2x - 6 \geqslant 2$ (b) $5x + 7 < 2x - 14$

2 Solve each of these inequalities. Represent the solution on a number line.

(a) $5 > 4x - 3 \geqslant x + 12$ (b) $2(x + 1) > x > 3(2x - 5)$

3 Factorise these quadratic expressions.

(a) $y^2 - 5y + 6$ (b) $p^2 + 2p - 24$ (c) $x^2 - 16$

4 Solve these quadratic equations by factorisation.

(a) $x^2 + 9x - 10 = 0$ (b) $x^2 = 9x - 14$

* 5 This triangle has an area of 48 cm².

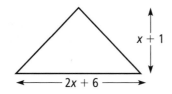

(a) Construct an equation, involving x, for the area of the triangle.
(b) Solve the equation to find the value of x.
(c) Use your solution to (b) to find the base length and height of the triangle.

* 6 A rectangle has a length and a width of
$2x$ and x respectively (in centimetres).
A square of side $(x - 1)$ is cut out of one
of its corners as shown.

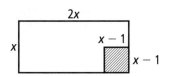

The area of the remaining shape is $7\ \text{cm}^2$.

(a) Write an expression for the area of the rectangle.
(b) Write an expression for the area of the removed square.
(c) Write an equation for the area of the remaining shape.
(d) Solve your equation in part (c) to find the value of x.

7 Calculate the volume of each of these spheres. Give your answers to
1 decimal place.

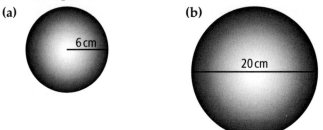

(a)

6 cm

(b)

20 cm

* 8 A hemisphere has a volume of $5000\ \text{cm}^3$. Calculate the size of its radius.
Give your answer correct to 2 decimal places.

9 A ladder 5 m long is placed against the side of a
building. The foot of the ladder is 1.5 m from the wall.
Calculate:

(a) the height h (in m) that the ladder reaches up
the side of the building
(b) the angle x (in degrees) that the foot of the ladder
makes with the ground.

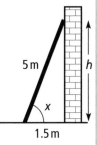

5 m

h

x

1.5 m

10 A boy standing at a point X is in line with two trees. The angle of
elevation of both tips of the trees from the boy is $20°$.

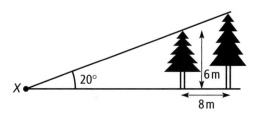

X

$20°$

6 m

8 m

If the height of the smaller tree is 6 m and the trees are 8 m apart,
calculate:

(a) the distance of the smaller tree from X
(b) the height of the taller tree.

Review 4B

1 Solve these inequalities.
(a) $5x + 6 < 16$ **(b)** $8x - 2 \geqslant 6x + 9$

2 Solve each of these inequalities. Represent the solution on a number line.
(a) $x - 4 \leqslant 2x + 1 \leqslant x + 12$ **(b)** $2x - 6 \geqslant x + 1 > 3(x - 4)$

3 Factorise these quadratic expressions.
(a) $x^2 + 7x - 8$ **(b)** $r^2 + r - 56$ **(c)** $p^2 + 10p + 25$

4 Solve these quadratic equations by factorisation.
(a) $x^2 - 13x + 36 = 0$ **(b)** $y^2 = 1$

*5 This parallelogram has an area of 30 cm².
(a) Construct an equation, involving x, for the area of the parallelogram.
(b) Solve the equation to find the value of x.
(c) Use your solution to **(b)** to find the base length and perpendicular height of the parallelogram.

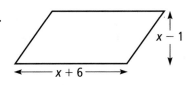

*6 A square and a rectangle have dimensions as shown.

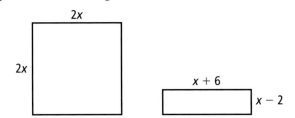

The area of the square is three times that of the rectangle.
(a) Write an expression for the area of the square.
(b) Write an expression for the area of the rectangle.
(c) Write an equation linking the areas of the square and the rectangle.
(d) Solve the equation to find the value of x.
(e) Use your solution to part **(d)** to calculate the dimensions of the square and the rectangle.

7 Calculate the volume of each of the following spheres. Give your answers to 3 significant figures.
(a) **(b)**

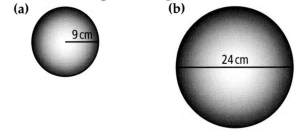

* **8** Two spheres A and B are shown below.

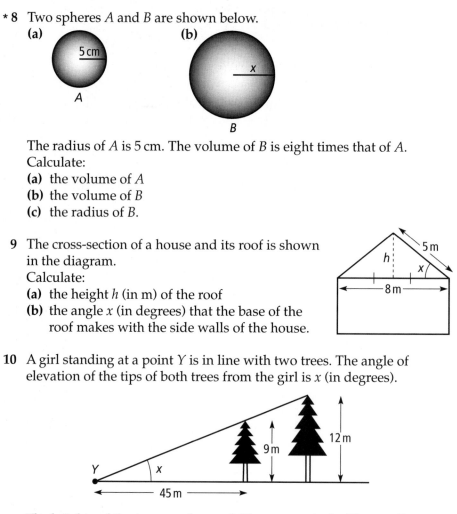

(a)   **(b)**

5 cm

A

x

B

The radius of A is 5 cm. The volume of B is eight times that of A.
Calculate:
(a) the volume of A
(b) the volume of B
(c) the radius of B.

9 The cross-section of a house and its roof is shown
in the diagram.
Calculate:
(a) the height h (in m) of the roof
(b) the angle x (in degrees) that the base of the
roof makes with the side walls of the house.

5 m

h

x

8 m

10 A girl standing at a point Y is in line with two trees. The angle of
elevation of the tips of both trees from the girl is x (in degrees).

12 m

9 m

Y

x

45 m

The heights of the trees are 9 m and 12 m respectively. The smaller tree is
45 m from Y. Calculate:
(a) the angle of elevation x (in degrees)
(b) the distance (in m) between the two trees.

Revision

The checkpoint framework has now been covered. Books 1, 2 and 3 have more than 60 chapters.

This revision section has a short test on each section of the three books. These should help you to identify those parts of the course which you will need to revise further.

Some advice on answering exam questions is given on page iii.

SECTION FIVE

Book 1

Section 1

1 Round each of these to 2 decimal places.
(a) 7.929
(b) 0.0063
(c) 1.097

2 Round each of these to 2 significant figures.
(a) 6842
(b) 36 500
(c) $3\frac{3}{4}$ million

3 Estimate the answer to:
(a) 48.5×310
(b) $8400 \div 21.4$

4 Solve these equations.
(a) $15 = a - 5$
(b) $13b = 52$
(c) $\dfrac{c}{5} = -2$

5 Draw these angles accurately.
(a) $52°$
(b) $128°$
(c) $105°$
(d) $75°$

6 (a) Construct a triangle ABC where

$AB = 8.5\,\text{cm}$ $AC = 6.2\,\text{cm}$ $BC = 5\,\text{cm}$

(b) Measure the angles at A, B and C.

7 A survey is taken to see how students travel to school. The following results are obtained.

Walk	Cycle	Bus	Car
130	50	300	60

Illustrate the results on a pie chart.

8 The numbers of litres of milk consumed per day in a sample of 100 homes are shown in this table.

Number of litres	1	2	3	4	5	6
Frequency	15	43	20	12	8	2

Illustrate this data on a suitable frequency chart.

9 The numbers of sweets in 50 packets of sweets are as shown below.

Sweets per packet	35	36	37	38	39	40
Frequency	3	5	7	15	12	8

Illustrate the data using a frequency chart.

10 In a survey, 540 English children were asked to vote for their favourite holiday destination. The results are shown in this table.

Destination	France	Spain	Portugal	Greece	Egypt	Italy	USA	Other
Frequency	108	120	54	36	30	27	63	102

Illustrate this data on a suitable pie chart.

Section 2

1 Without using a calculator, find these square roots.
   (a) $\sqrt{49}$ (b) $\sqrt{400}$ (c) $\sqrt{169}$

2 Without using a calculator, calculate:
   (a) 2.5^2 (b) 0.5^2 (c) $\sqrt{0.49}$

3 Write down all the prime numbers between 20 and 50.

4 Write down the prime factors of 350.

5 What is the lowest common multiple of 4, 6 and 10?

6 What is the highest common factor of 42, 126 and 210?

7 Write down the next two terms of each of these sequences.
   (a) 2, 6, 10, 14   (b) 8, 17, 26, 35, 44
   (c) 90, 81, 72, 63   (d) 1, 4, 9, 16, 25

8 Give an expression for the nth term of each of these sequences.
   (a) 4, 7, 10, 13   (b) 4, 9, 14, 19, 24

9 (a) On a suitable grid, plot these points.
       $A = (4, 3)$ $B = (2, -2)$ $C = (-3, -2)$ $D = (-4, 3)$
   (b) Name the shape formed by joining $ABCD$.

* 10 The numbers of people attending a swimming pool each day in March were as shown below.

162	85	46	52	68	144	79	105	118	136	157
44	83	77	62	85	131	70	68	152	123	132
67	76	49	63	87	99	101	141	78		

   (a) Write the data in a grouped frequency table.
   (b) Draw a histogram to illustrate the data.

Section 3

1 Evaluate these.
   (a) $\frac{3}{4}$ of 480   (b) $\frac{3}{16}$ of 120   (c) $\frac{7}{9}$ of 63   (d) $\frac{4}{11}$ of 176

2 Evaluate these.
   (a) $\frac{1}{2} + \frac{1}{4} + \frac{1}{3}$ (b) $\frac{7}{8} + \frac{1}{4} - \frac{9}{16}$ (c) $2\frac{1}{4} - 7\frac{7}{8}$

3 Convert each of these to a percentage.

(a) $\frac{3}{5}$ (b) $\frac{5}{8}$ (c) 0.17 (d) 1.4

4 Convert each of these to a decimal.

(a) $\frac{1}{8}$ (b) $\frac{4}{5}$ (c) 45% (d) 160%

5 Plot these straight-line graphs.

(a) $y = 2x$ (b) $y = x - 3$

*   **6** Write down the equation of each of these straight lines.

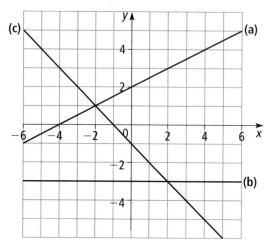

7 Copy each of these diagrams and draw the reflection of the shape in the mirror line.

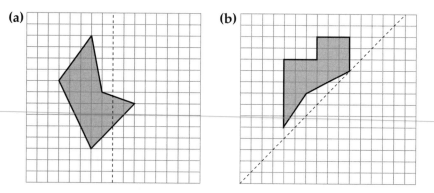

8 A pattern has rotational symmetry of order 6. Calculate the angle between adjacent images.

9 A bag contains 15 red, 4 blue and 6 green counters. What is the probability of the first counter drawn being:

(a) red or blue (b) green (c) white?

10 I have two tickets for a football match. This represents 0.000 05 of the total tickets sold. How many tickets were sold?

Section 4

1 Evaluate:
(a) 25% of 240   (b) 45% of 500   (c) $62\frac{1}{2}$% of 80

2 (a) Increase 160 by 25%.
   (b) Decrease 320 by 20%.
   (c) Increase 50 by 150%.

3 A shop is having a sale. A coat costing €150 is discounted by 30%. What is its sale price?

4 A teacher's salary increases by 4%. If her previous salary was €24 000, what is her new salary?

5 Expand each of these expressions.
   (a) $4(a - 3)$ (b) $-5(3b - 7)$
   (c) $c(2b + 4)$ (d) $3a(4a - 3b + c)$

6 Expand each of these expressions.
   (a) $(a + b)(a - b)$ (b) $(p + q)^2$
   (c) $(2m - 3)(n - 4)$ (d) $(m - n)^2$

7 (a) On a co-ordinate grid, draw the following triangle with its vertices at the points given.

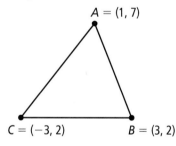

$A = (1, 7)$

$C = (-3, 2)$ $B = (3, 2)$

   (b) Enlarge the triangle by a scale factor of 2 from point D at $(0, 2)$.

8 Find the mean, median and mode of the following data.
   4 2 1 3 3 1 1 2 4 2 3 2 1
   1 5 2 3 4 2 1 3 2 5 1 4

9 An athlete keeps a record of her training times for the 100 m race:
   14.0   13.6   13.1   13.2   13.4   13.0   13.6   13.2
   What are the mean and the range of her training times?

* 10 Sixty flowering bushes are planted. At the time when they have most flowers, the number of flowers on each bush is counted and recorded. The results are shown in this table.

Flowers per bush	0	1	2	3	4	5	6	7	8	9	10	11	12
Frequency	0	0	0	0	0	1	2	4	10	5	10	12	16

   Calculate the mean and the median numbers of flowers.

Section 5

1   A model car is made to a scale of $1:40$. The actual car is 5.4 m long. How long is the model car?

2   Divide 60 in the ratio $2:3:5$.

3   The ratio of the angles of a quadrilateral is $2:2:3:1$. What is the size of each angle?

4   Evaluate each of these expressions when $a = 2$, $b = 3$ and $c = 4$.
  (a) $3a - 2b + 4c$ **(b)** $a^2 + b^2 - c^2$

5   Using a pair of compasses, construct an isosceles triangle ABC, where $AB = 5$ cm and $AC = BC = 7.5$ cm.

6   Calculate the area of this parallelogram.

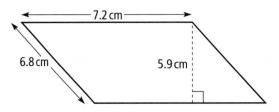

7   Calculate the area of this trapezium.

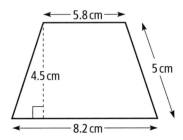

* 8   What is the probability of throwing a total of 7 when two fair dice are thrown?

Book 2

Section 1

1 A train journey takes 2 hours 15 minutes. Copy and complete the timetable below.

Depart	0600	0815		1308		
Arrive			1235		1805	2120

2 Use a calculator to find the answers to these.
   (a) $-8.3 - 7.9 + 4.6$ (b) 4.8×-3.5 (c) $46 \div -2.3$

3 Copy each of these calculations and add brackets to make it correct.
   (a) $4 + 2 \times 6 = 36$ (b) $8 + 2 \times 5 - 3 = 20$ (c) $5 - 3 \times 9 + 2 \div 2 = 11$

4 Work out these without using a calculator.

   (a) $8 + \dfrac{4}{4}$ (b) $16 + \dfrac{10}{7 - 2}$ (c) $\dfrac{15 + 25}{2 \times 5}$

5 Draw a circle, and mark and label the following on it.
   (a) A radius   (b) A tangent   (c) A minor arc   (d) A sector

6 Construct a regular hexagon of side 5 cm.

7 Draw a line 9 cm long and construct its perpendicular bisector.

8 Suggest four questions that could be used in a survey to find out the reading habits of pupils in your class.

Section 2

1 Convert these to metres.
   (a) 8950 cm   (b) 0.7 km   (c) 45 cm

2 Convert these to kilograms.
   (a) 3 tonnes   (b) 0.05 tonne   (c) 750 g

3 Convert these to millilitres.
   (a) 0.06 litres   (b) 4.2 litres   (c) 0.008 litres

4 Solve these equations.
   (a) $4 + 3a = 19$ (b) $4b - 2 = 2b + 8$ (c) $5(c - 3) = c + 1$

5 Calculate the circumference of a circle of radius:
   (a) 8 cm   (b) 3.6 cm

6 Calculate the circumference of a circle of diameter:
   (a) 12 cm   (b) 14.4 cm

7 Calculate the area of a circle of radius:
(a) 5 cm   (b) 3.8 cm

8 Calculate the shaded area of this disc.

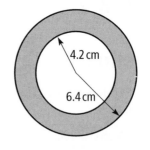

9 Draw a possible net for this cuboid.

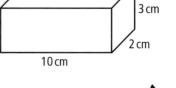

10 Draw a possible net for this square-based pyramid.

Section 3

1 Write each of these inequalities in words.
(a) $a < 8$ (b) $b > 6$ (c) $c \neq 5$ (d) $d \leqslant 11$

2 Rewrite each of these using the correct inequality sign(s).
(a) a is less than b
(b) b is more than 4 but less than 12
(c) c is greater than or equal to b, but less than d.

3 Show each of these inequalities on a number line.
(a) $a < 6$ (b) $b \geqslant 9$ (c) $7 \leqslant c \leqslant 11$

4 Rearrange each of these formulae to make x the subject.
(a) $p = x - 3$ (b) $4(x - y) = 2z$ (c) $3 + \dfrac{m}{l} = \dfrac{1}{x}$

5 Rearrange each of these formulae to make y the subject.
(a) $4m = 3n - 2y$ (b) $2p = y^2 - q$ (c) $\dfrac{x}{y} = \dfrac{p}{q}$

* 6 Explain what is meant by a line of best fit on a scatter graph. Use a diagram in your explanation.

* 7 Draw a scatter diagram to show:
(a) weak positive correlation
(b) strong negative correlation.

8 Calculate angle x in each of these diagrams.

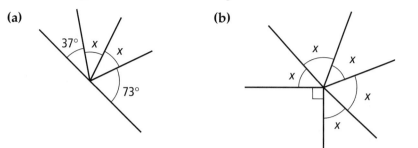

(a) **(b)**

9 Calculate the unknown angles in these diagrams.

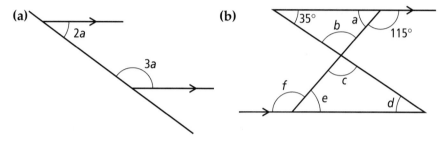

(a) **(b)**

10 'All rhombuses are parallelograms, but not all parallelograms are rhombuses.' With the aid of diagrams, explain this statement.

Section 4

1 A principal sum of €1200 is invested. Using the formula $I = \dfrac{ptr}{100}$ calculate the yearly rate of simple interest that will earn a total of €100 interest after four years. Give your answer correct to 1 decimal place.

2 Given the following cost prices and selling prices of a number of items, calculate the percentage profit or loss in each case.
   (a) Cost price = €90   Selling price = €100
   (b) Cost price = €650   Selling price = €625
   (c) Cost price = €40   Selling price = €100

3 Factorise each of these expressions.
   (a) $6a + 12$ **(b)** $15a + 18b - 6c$ **(c)** $21x - 56y$

4 Factorise each of these expressions.
   (a) $3ab + 6a^2$ **(b)** $18x^2y^3 + 12x^2y$ **(c)** $36a^2b^3 + 27ab^2z - 9a^2bz$

* 5 Factorise each of these expressions by grouping.
   (a) $2xa + 2xb + 3a + 3b$
   (b) $4yp + zp - 8yq - 2zq$

* **6** Calculate the volume of this cylinder. Give your answer to 1 decimal place.

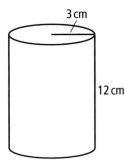

* **7** This triangular prism has a volume of 240 cm³.
  Calculate the prism's height, h.

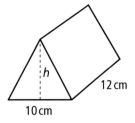

* **8** A square sheet of metal, of side length 11 cm and thickness 2 mm, has a smaller square of side length x (in cm) cut from it.

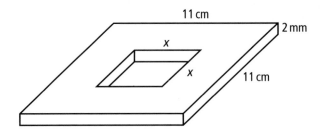

  If the volume of the remaining shape is 17 cm³, calculate the value of x.

* **9** A bag contains 3 white balls, 8 green balls and 4 blue balls. Calculate the probability that the first ball picked is:

  (a) white   **(b)** blue   **(c)** white or blue.

* **10** A box contains six triangular tokens and six circular tokens, numbered as shown.

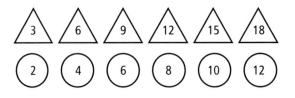

  If a token is picked out of the box at random, calculate the probability that:
  (a) it is circular
  (b) the number is a multiple of 3
  (c) the number is prime.

Section 5

1 Deduce the equation of each of these straight lines.

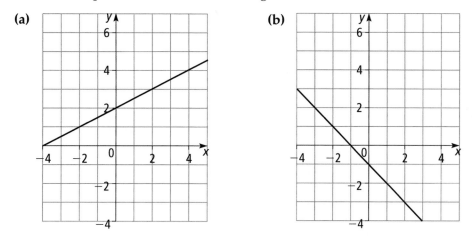

(a)

(b)

2 On a co-ordinate grid, draw the straight line represented by each of these equations.
   (a) $y = 3x - 4$ (b) $2y - 4x = -4$

* 3 Calculate the gradient of the line passing through each of these pairs of points.
   (a) $(1, 0)$ and $(3, 8)$ (b) $(2, 5)$ and $(8, 2)$

4 Calculate the size of each exterior angle of a regular pentagon.

5 Calculate the size of angle a in this heptagon.

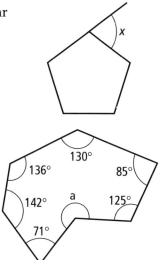

6 This diagram shows part of a regular polygon. The size of each interior angle is 168°.

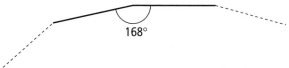

168°

Calculate the number of sides that the regular polygon has.

* **7** Calculate the surface area of this cuboid.

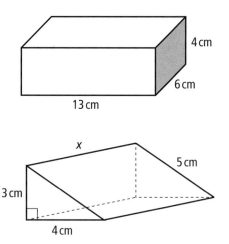

* **8** This triangular prism has a total surface area of 120 cm².

Calculate the value of x (in cm).

* **9** This frequency table shows the heights of 60 girls in a school year.

Height (cm)	130–	140–	150–	160–	170–180
Frequency	7	12	28	10	3

Show these results on a frequency polygon.

* **10** Two classes of 30 pupils take the same maths test. One class has a mixture of pupils of different abilities. The other is a class where pupils have similar mathematical abilities. Their percentage scores are shown in this table.

Percentage	0–	20–	40–	60–	80–100
Class A frequency	2	24	4	0	0
Class B frequency	7	6	5	5	7

(a) On the same grid, plot a frequency polygon for each class.
(b) From your graph, deduce which class is more likely to be the mixed ability class. Give reasons for your answer.

Book 3

Section 1

1 Simplify these.
   (a) $5^3 \times 5^2$ (b) $8^3 \div 8^3$ (c) $(2^3)^2$

2 Simplify these.
   (a) $a \times a \times b \times b \times b \times c$ (b) $p^9 \div p^3$

3 Find the value of each of these.
   (a) $3^7 \div 3^5$ (b) $a^6 \div a^5$

4 A car travels 320 km in 8 hours. What is its average speed?

5 How far will a boy cycle in 90 minutes at 12 km/h?

6 A stone has a volume of 350 cm³ and a density of 5.8 g/cm³. What is its mass?

7 Find the length of AC in this diagram.

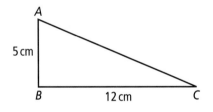

8 Find the length of side BC in this triangle.

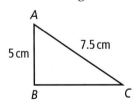

9 Find the length of side AB in this triangle.

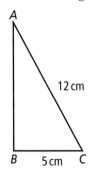

10 Draw this diagram accurately, using a scale of 1 cm = 10 km.

    (a) Measure the lengths of *AB* and *BC* and give their true lengths in kilometres.

    (b) Measure the bearing of *C* from *B*.

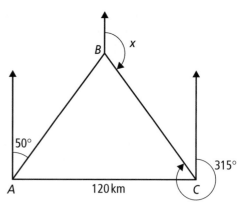

Section 2

1 Write these in standard form.

    (a) $7\frac{1}{2}$ million   **(b)** 6 billion

2 Multiply each of these and give your answer in standard form.

    (a) 5000×400 **(b)** $(7000)^2$

3 Calculate these and give your answers in standard form.

    (a) $(2.8 \times 10^5)^2$ **(b)** $(7.2 \times 10^9) \div (1.8 \times 10^3)$

* **4** Write these in standard form.

    (a) $0.000\,000\,617$ **(b)** $\frac{3}{100\,000}$

5 Solve each of these pairs of simultaneous equations.

    (a) $3p - 4q = -5$ **(b)** $m + n = 13$
         $3p + 4q = 11$ $2m - 3n = 1$

* **6** Find the values of x and y in this equilateral triangle.

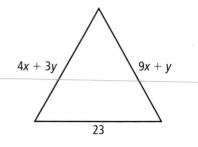

7 Find the length of the side marked x in this diagram.

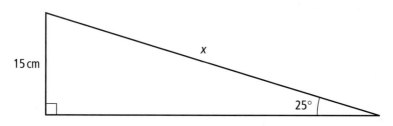

8 Find the length of the side marked x in this diagram.

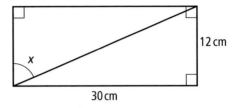

9 Find the size of the angle marked x in this diagram.

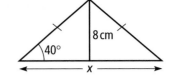

10 The boiling point of water is 100° Celsius and 373 kelvins.
Absolute zero is −273° Celsius and 0 kelvin.
At what temperature does water freeze, in kelvins?

Section 3

1 A girl's height is given as 162 cm to the nearest centimetre.
   (a) Write down the lower and upper bounds within which her height can lie.
   (b) Represent this range of numbers on a number line.
   (c) If the girl's height is h cm, express this range as an inequality.

2 A boy's time to run a 100 m race is given as 13.9 seconds, correct to 1 decimal place.
   (a) Write down the lower and upper bounds within which his time can lie.
   (b) Represent this range of numbers on a number line.
   (c) If the boy's time is t seconds, express this range as an inequality.

3 Solve each of these pairs of simultaneous equations graphically.
   (a) $y = x - 4$ (b) $y + 2x = -6$
       $y = -x + 4$ $y - 4 = 0$

* 4 The lines represented by these two simultaneous equations intersect at the point where the x co-ordinate is 2.

   $y + x = 5$
   $y - mx = 2$

   (a) Calculate the y co-ordinate of the point of intersection.
   (b) Calculate the value of m.
   (c) Plot both lines on the same grid and use your graph to confirm your solution to part (a).

5 **(a)** Plot the lines represented by these simultaneous equations on the same grid.

$y = 3x - 2$
$y = 3x + 2$

(b) In your own words describe your graph.
(c) How many solutions are there?
(d) Explain your answer to part **(c)**.

6 Using trigonometry, calculate the value of x in each of these right-angled triangles.

(a)   **(b)**

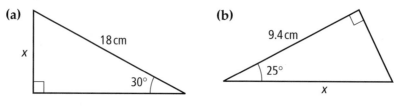

7 Calculate the size of the angle marked a in each of these right-angled triangles. Give your answers to the nearest whole number.

(a)   **(b)**

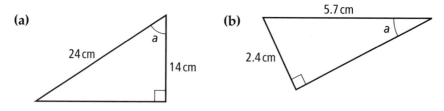

* 8 Using trigonometry, deduce whether angle x is a right angle.

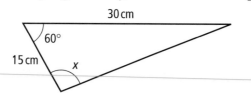

9 A garden 10 m by 15 m has two sprinklers at A and B as shown.

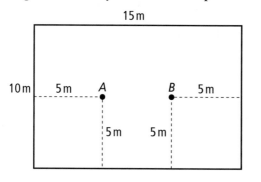

Sprinkler A has a range of 6 m. Sprinkler B has a range of 4 m.
(a) Draw a scale diagram of the garden.
(b) Draw the locus of all the points that can be reached by sprinkler A.
(c) Draw the locus of all the points that can be reached by sprinkler B.
(d) Shade the locus of points that can be reached by both A and B.

10 Points X and Y are 8 cm apart.

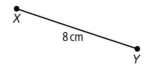

(a) Make a scale copy of the diagram.
(b) Construct the locus of all the points that are equidistant from both X and
     Y but also no further than 8 cm from either.

Section 4

1 Solve these inequalities.
   (a) $2x - 4 \leqslant x + 2$ (b) $3(x + 2) > x - 4$

* 2 Solve each of these inequalities and represent the solution on a number line.
   (a) $7x + 4 \leqslant 2x - 6$ (b) $3x + 4 \leqslant 5x - 2 < 2(2x + 5)$

   (c) $\dfrac{-6x + 2}{4} \geqslant 5$

3 Factorise these quadratic expressions.
   (a) $x^2 + 2x - 15$ (b) $x^2 - 10x + 21$

4 Solve these quadratic equations by factorisation.
   (a) $x^2 + 5x - 6 = 0$ (b) $2x^2 - 5x + 8 = x^2 + 3x - 8$

5 This rectangle has an area of 28 cm².
   (a) Form an equation for the area of
       the rectangle, involving x.
   (b) Solve your equation to find the
       values of x.
   (c) Calculate the length and width of the rectangle.

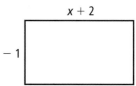

6 This triangle has an area of 100 cm².
   (a) Write an equation for the area of
       the triangle, involving x.
   (b) Solve the equation to find the
       value of x.
   (c) Calculate the base length and
       height of the triangle.

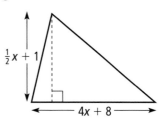

7 Calculate the volume of a sphere with radius 10 cm.

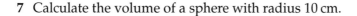

* **8** A hollow rubber ball is used for a game of football in a school playground. The exterior radius of the ball is 12 cm. The thickness of the rubber is 4 mm.
Calculate the volume of rubber used in making the ball.

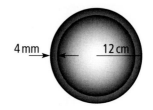

9 A rectangular school field *ABCD* is 150 m wide and 220 m long as shown.

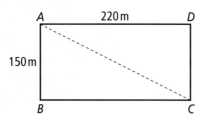

A pupil decides to run the triangular route *ABC*. Calculate:
(a) the length *AC*
(b) the number of complete routes he will do if he runs 5 km.

10 A footbridge crosses a canal as shown.

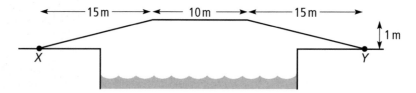

The height of the horizontal section of the footbridge above ground level is 1 m. Calculate:
(a) the angle that the sloping part of the footbridge makes with the ground
(b) the distance a person has to walk to get from point *X* at the start of the footbridge to the point *Y* at the other end. Give your answer to the nearest centimetre.

Extension

SECTION SIX

Reverse percentages

If you are given the selling price of an item and the percentage profit, it is possible to work backwards and find the cost price. One way is to use the unitary method.

Worked examples

(i) A new car is sold for €12 000, making a 20% profit for the car dealer. What did the car cost the dealer?

The profit is 20%. Therefore the selling price is 120% of the cost price.

> 120% of the cost price is €12 000
> therefore 1% of the cost price is €12 000 ÷ 120 = €100
> 100% of the cost price is €100 × 100

The cost price is €10 000.

(ii) A maths text book has 98 pages of algebra. This is 35% of the book. How many pages are there in the book?

> 35% of the book is 98 pages
> so 1% of the book is 98 ÷ 35 pages
> therefore 100% of the book is 98 ÷ 35 × 100 pages

The book has 280 pages.

EXERCISE 21.1

Calculate the value of C in each of these.

1	7% of C is 210	**2**	20% of C is 240
3	48% of C is 168	**4**	15% of C is 75
5	4% of C is 100	**6**	85% of C is 765
7	10% of C is 2	**8**	50% of C is 5.5
9	12% of C is 43.2	**10**	75% of C is 420

EXERCISE 21.2

Calculate the value of *D* in each of these.

1   150% of *D* is 240   2   125% of *D* is 140
3   110% of *D* is 396   4   175% of *D* is 385
5   140% of *D* is 89.6   6   125% of *D* is 80
7   144% of *D* is 109.44   8   125% of *D* is 88
9   250% of *D* is 5   10   103% of *D* is 618

EXERCISE 21.3

1   In a test, Ahmed answered 92% of the questions correctly. If he answered 46 questions correctly, how many questions were there?

2   A boat is sold for €7680, making a profit of 28%. What was the original price?

3   In a class, 28% of students have a computer. The number of students with a computer is 35. How many students are there in the class?

4   Ayse gets 88% in a test. She got six questions wrong. How many did she get correct?

5   A car company sells 3840 cars, which is a 20% increase in sales over the previous year. How many were sold in the previous year?

6   A house is sold for €240 000. This represents a 60% profit over ten years. What did the house cost the owner ten years ago?

7   A car is sold for €3000 after five years. This represents a 60% loss. What did the car cost originally?

8   In a test, Peter gets 75%. He answered 30 of the questions wrongly. How many questions were there?

9   An antique dealer makes 10% profit on a chair. If he sold it for €396, what did it cost him?

10   A woman makes a profit of 8% on the sale of a bicycle. She sold it for €378. What did it cost?

EXERCISE 21.4

Mixed percentages
Do not use a calculator.

1   Calculate each of these percentages.
    (a) 25% of 240   **(b)** 70% of 300
    (c) $12\frac{1}{2}$% of 160   **(d)** $66\frac{2}{3}$% of 180

2   Increase each of these amounts by the given percentage.
    (a) 640 by 25%   **(b)** 250 by 20%
    (c) 320 by $12\frac{1}{2}$%   **(d)** 80 by 67.5%

3   Decrease each of these amounts by the given percentage.
    (a) 250 by 30%   **(b)** 640 by 12.5%
    (c) 330 by $33\frac{1}{3}$%   **(d)** 880 by $87\frac{1}{2}$%

4 Find the simple interest on a deposit of €240 after 5 years at 7%.

5 How long will it take to earn €600 in simple interest on a deposit of €2000 invested at 5%?

6 A car cost €8000 and is sold for €6000. What is the percentage loss?

7 An antique table cost €400 and is sold ten years later for €1000. What is the percentage profit?

8 A car is sold for €6000, making a 20% profit. What was its cost price?

9 A girl scores 80% in an examination. If she had ten incorrect answers, how many were correct?

10 A square is doubled in area. What is the percentage increase in its area?

Solving quadratic equations graphically

In Chapter 17, you learned that it was possible to solve quadratic equations using factors. There are times, however, when a quadratic equation cannot be factorised and yet still has a solution. Another way of solving quadratic equations is by graphing them.

Worked examples

(i) Solve the quadratic equation $x^2 + 4x + 3 = 0$:
   (a) using factors   **(b)** graphically.

   (a) $x^2 + 4x + 3$ can be factorised to give $(x + 1)(x + 3)$.
   When $(x + 1)(x + 3) = 0$, either $x + 1 = 0$ or $x + 3 = 0$.
   Therefore $x = -1$ or -3.

   (b) To solve the equation $x^2 + 4x + 3 = 0$ graphically, plot the graph of $y = x^2 + 4x + 3$.
   First produce a table of results for a range of x values.
   Then use these x and y values to plot points on the graph.

x	y
-4	3
-3	0
-2	-1
-1	0
0	3
1	8

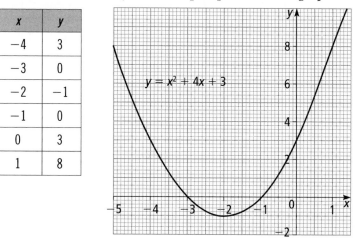

$y = x^2 + 4x + 3$

   To solve the equation $x^2 + 4x + 3 = 0$ from the graph $y = x^2 + 4x + 3$, check where the graph cuts the x axis, as it is at these points that $y = 0$. From the graph it can be seen that the curve cuts the x axis when $x = -1$ and -3.
   The solutions are the same as when solving by factors – as expected!

(ii) Solve the following quadratic equation.

   $$x^2 - 4x + 1 = 0$$

This quadratic equation cannot be factorised. However, by plotting a graph of $y = x^2 - 4x + 1$ we can see where it crosses the x axis.

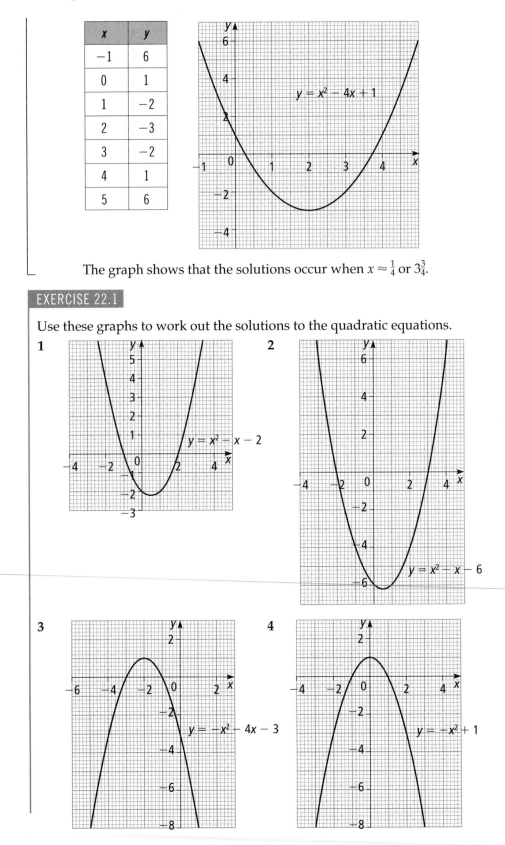

x	y
−1	6
0	1
1	−2
2	−3
3	−2
4	1
5	6

$y = x^2 - 4x + 1$

The graph shows that the solutions occur when $x \approx \frac{1}{4}$ or $3\frac{3}{4}$.

EXERCISE 22.1

Use these graphs to work out the solutions to the quadratic equations.

1 $y = x^2 - x - 2$

2 $y = x^2 - x - 6$

3 $y = -x^2 - 4x - 3$

4 $y = -x^2 + 1$

5 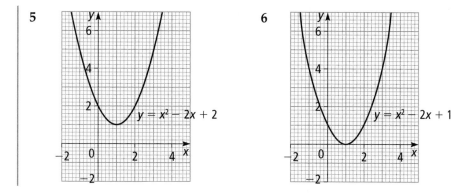   **6**

EXERCISE 22.2

You will need graph paper for this exercise.

For each of the following quadratic equations:
(a) complete a table of results for the range of x values given
(b) plot a graph to represent the equation
(c) deduce from the graph the solution(s) to the equation.

1	$x^2 - 5x + 6 = 0$	range $0 \leqslant x \leqslant 5$
2	$x^2 - 4 = 0$	range $-3 \leqslant x \leqslant 3$
3	$x^2 - 4\frac{1}{2}x + 2 = 0$	range $-1 \leqslant x \leqslant 5$
4	$-x^2 + x + 6 = 0$	range $-3 \leqslant x \leqslant 4$
5	$x^2 + 6x + 9 = 0$	range $-6 \leqslant x \leqslant 0$
6	$4x^2 - 16x + 14 = 0$	range $0 \leqslant x \leqslant 4$
7	$-3x^2 + 4x = 0$	range $-1 \leqslant x \leqslant 2$
8	$-x^2 + 3x - 3 = 0$	range $-1 \leqslant x \leqslant 4$

Quadratic equations can be produced from real situations. In the examples below, the equations need to be constructed first, using the information given, before they can be solved.

Worked examples

(i) A rectangle has an area of 30 cm². Its length and width are $(x + 3)$ cm and $(x - 1)$ cm respectively, as shown.

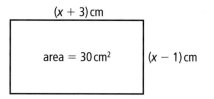

$(x + 3)$ cm

area = 30 cm² $(x - 1)$ cm

(a) Form an equation for the area of the rectangle.
(b) Plot a graph and use it to solve the equation.

(a) The equation is given by length × width = area.

$$(x + 3)(x - 1) = 30$$
$$x^2 + 2x - 3 = 30$$
$$x^2 + 2x - 33 = 0$$

(b)

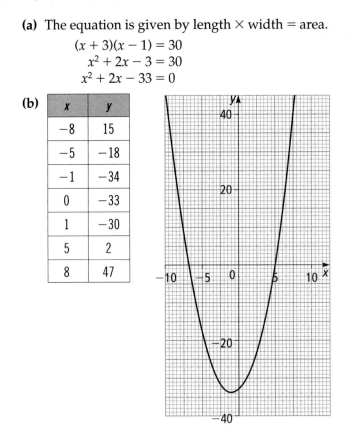

x	y
−8	15
−5	−18
−1	−34
0	−33
1	−30
5	2
8	47

From the graph it can be seen that there are two values of x which make $x^2 + 2x - 33 = 0$ (i.e. two places where the curve cuts the x axis). Therefore $x \approx -6.8$ or $x \approx 4.8$. However, if $x = -6.8$ then both the length and width of the rectangle will be negative, which is a nonsensical solution.

Therefore $x \approx 4.8$ is the solution.

(ii) Two circles, A and B, have radii of r cm and $(r + 4)$ cm respectively. The area of circle B is twice that of A.

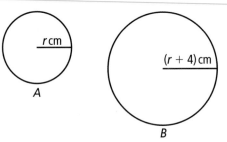

(a) Form an expression for the area of each circle.
(b) Form an equation showing the relationship between the areas of the two circles.
(c) Plot a graph to represent the equation and use it to give an approximate solution for the value of r.

(a) The area of A is πr^2.

The area of B is $\pi(r + 4)^2$.

(b) As the area of B is twice that of A:

$$2\pi r^2 = \pi(r + 4)^2$$
$$2r^2 = (r + 4)^2$$
$$2r^2 = r^2 + 8r + 16$$

Therefore $r^2 - 8r - 16 = 0$

(c)

r	-2	-1	0	1	4	8	10
y	4	-7	-16	-23	-32	-16	4

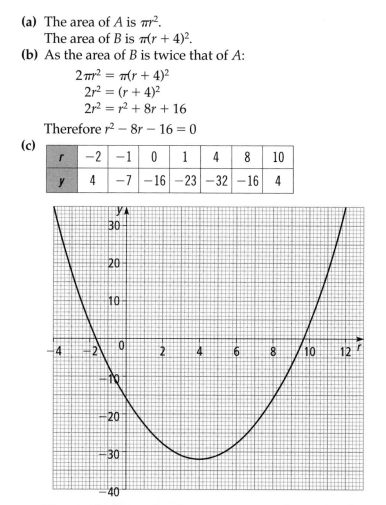

The graph shows that the curve crosses the r axis when $r \approx -1.7$ and when $r \approx 9.7$.

As the negative value of r produces a negative radius for circle A, the solution must be $r \approx 9.7$.

Therefore the radius of circle $A \approx 9.7$ cm and the radius of circle $B \approx 13.7$ cm.

EXERCISE 22.3

You will need graph paper for this exercise.

1 The area of a rectangle is 20 cm². Its length and width are $(x + 5)$ cm and $(x + 2)$ cm respectively.

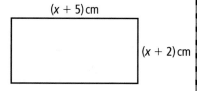

(a) Form an equation for the area of the rectangle, involving x.

(b) Plot a graph to represent the equation and use it to find an approximate value for x.

(c) What are the length and width of the rectangle?

2   Two squares A and B are shown in the diagram.
Square A has a side length of m cm; B has a side length of $(2m - 2)$ cm. The area of B is three times that of A.

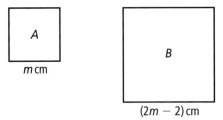

(a) Write an expression for the area of each square.
(b) Form an equation linking the areas of the two squares.
(c) Plot a graph of the equation and use it to find an approximate value for m.
(d) What is the length of each side of square B?

3   Two cubes P and Q are shown in the diagram. The side lengths of P and Q are x cm and $(x + 2)$ cm respectively.

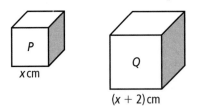

(a) Write an expression for the total surface area of P.
(b) Write an expression for the total surface area of Q.

The total surface area of Q is twice that of P.

(c) Form an equation linking the total surface areas of P and Q.
(d) Plot a graph to represent the equation and use it to work out an approximate value for x.

4   The square and triangle shown have the same area.

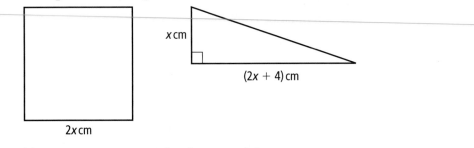

(a) Write an expression for the area of the square.
(b) Write an expression for the area of the triangle.
(c) Form an equation linking the areas of the two shapes.
(d) Plot a graph to represent the equation and use it to find an approximate value for x.
(e) Use your solution for x to give an estimate for the dimensions of each shape.

5 Two circles X and Y have radii $(r - 1)$ cm and $(r + 5)$ cm respectively, as shown. The area of Y is three times that of X.

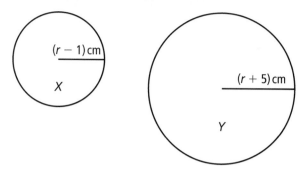

(a) Form an equation linking the areas of X and Y.

(b) Plot a graph to represent the equation and use it to find an approximate value for r.

(c) What are the approximate lengths of the radii of the circles X and Y?

6 This cube and cuboid have dimensions as shown. The total surface area of the cube is twice that of the cuboid.

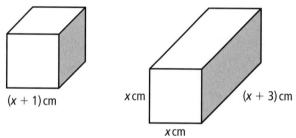

(a) Write an expression for the total surface area of the cube.

(b) Write an expression for the total surface area of the cuboid.

(c) Form an equation linking the areas of the two shapes.

(d) Plot a graph to represent the equation and use it to find an approximate value for x.

(e) Use your value of x to give an approximate value for the total surface area of the cuboid.

Shape, space and measures 10

Simple vectors

You will already be aware, from Book 1, of some types of transformation, such as reflection, rotation and translation. Translations represent a sliding motion that involves no rotation. In this chapter we look at a more mathematical way of describing translations.

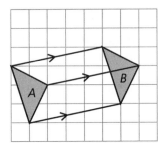

In this diagram, triangle *A* has been translated to position *B*. This translation can be described as a movement 5 units to the right and 1 unit up. Another way of describing this translation is to use **column vectors**. The column vector describing this translation is $\begin{pmatrix} 5 \\ 1 \end{pmatrix}$.

A column vector consists of two numbers written one above the other inside square or round brackets. The top number represents how far the object has moved horizontally, and the bottom number represents how far it has moved vertically.

Positive numbers mean a move either to the right or upwards, and negative numbers mean a translation to the left or downwards. For example,

$\begin{pmatrix} 3 \\ 7 \end{pmatrix}$ means a translation of 3 units to the *right* and 7 units vertically *upwards*

$\begin{pmatrix} -1 \\ -5 \end{pmatrix}$ means a translation of 1 unit to the *left* and 5 units vertically *downwards*

EXERCISE 23.1

Write each of these descriptions of translations as a column vector.
1   2 units to the *right* and 3 units vertically *upwards*
2   5 units to the *right* and 1 unit vertically *upwards*
3   4 units to the *left* and 2 units vertically *upwards*
4   6 units to the *right* and 3 units vertically *downwards*

5 2 units to the *left* and 7 units vertically *downwards*

6 0 units horizontally and 8 units vertically *downwards*

7 6 units to the *left* and 0 units vertically

8 0 units horizontally and 0 units vertically

EXERCISE 23.2

Write in words the translation represented by each of these column vectors.

1 $\begin{pmatrix} 4 \\ 4 \end{pmatrix}$
  2 $\begin{pmatrix} 1 \\ 0 \end{pmatrix}$
  3 $\begin{pmatrix} 2 \\ -9 \end{pmatrix}$
  4 $\begin{pmatrix} -6 \\ 5 \end{pmatrix}$

5 $\begin{pmatrix} -8 \\ -2 \end{pmatrix}$
  6 $\begin{pmatrix} 0 \\ -\frac{1}{2} \end{pmatrix}$
  7 $\begin{pmatrix} -4 \\ 0 \end{pmatrix}$
  8 $\begin{pmatrix} \frac{1}{2} \\ -10 \end{pmatrix}$

EXERCISE 23.3

You will need squared paper for this exercise.

1 This diagram shows a triangle *A*, translated to position *B*, then to positions *C*, *D*, *E* and back to *A*.
Write each of the following translations as a column vector.

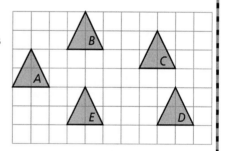

    (a) *A* to *B*
    (b) *B* to *C*
    (c) *C* to *D*
    (d) *D* to *E*
    (e) *E* to *A*

2 This diagram shows part of a repeating pattern on a sheet of wrapping paper.
Describe, using column vectors, the translation from:

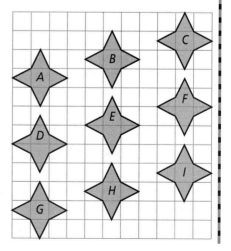

    (a) *A* to *B*
    (b) *B* to *A*
    (c) *D* to *F*
    (d) *E* to *I*
    (e) *A* to *H*
    (f) *C* to *G*
    (g) *B* to *H*
    (h) *I* to *F*

3 Copy this diagram.

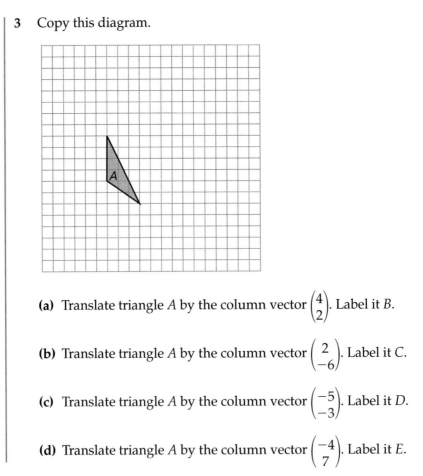

(a) Translate triangle A by the column vector $\begin{pmatrix} 4 \\ 2 \end{pmatrix}$. Label it B.

(b) Translate triangle A by the column vector $\begin{pmatrix} 2 \\ -6 \end{pmatrix}$. Label it C.

(c) Translate triangle A by the column vector $\begin{pmatrix} -5 \\ -3 \end{pmatrix}$. Label it D.

(d) Translate triangle A by the column vector $\begin{pmatrix} -4 \\ 7 \end{pmatrix}$. Label it E.

The diagram below shows a series of translations represented on a grid.

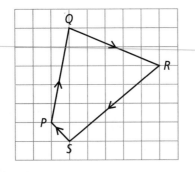

The translation from P to Q is $\begin{pmatrix} 1 \\ 5 \end{pmatrix}$. This can also be written as $\overrightarrow{PQ} = \begin{pmatrix} 1 \\ 5 \end{pmatrix}$

Similarly $\overrightarrow{QR} = \begin{pmatrix} 5 \\ -2 \end{pmatrix}$, $\overrightarrow{RS} = \begin{pmatrix} -5 \\ -4 \end{pmatrix}$ and $\overrightarrow{SP} = \begin{pmatrix} -1 \\ 1 \end{pmatrix}$

EXERCISE 23.4

For questions 1–3, describe each of the translations using a column vector.

1
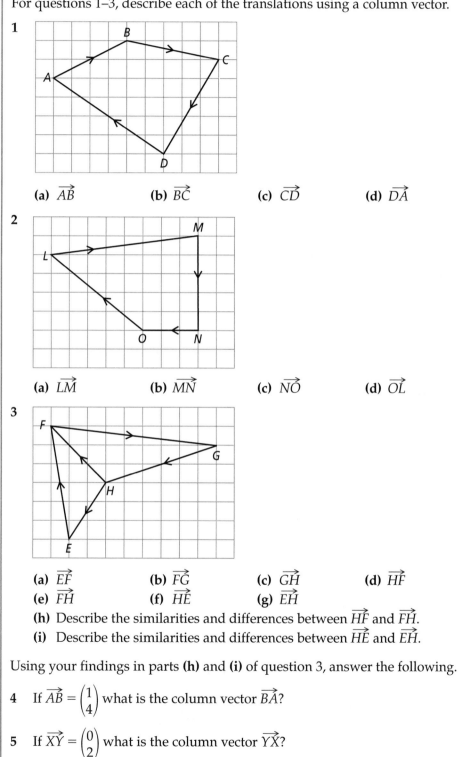

(a) $\overrightarrow{AB}$ (b) $\overrightarrow{BC}$ (c) $\overrightarrow{CD}$ (d) $\overrightarrow{DA}$

2

(a) $\overrightarrow{LM}$ (b) $\overrightarrow{MN}$ (c) $\overrightarrow{NO}$ (d) $\overrightarrow{OL}$

3

(a) $\overrightarrow{EF}$ (b) $\overrightarrow{FG}$ (c) $\overrightarrow{GH}$ (d) $\overrightarrow{HF}$
(e) $\overrightarrow{FH}$ (f) $\overrightarrow{HE}$ (g) $\overrightarrow{EH}$
(h) Describe the similarities and differences between $\overrightarrow{HF}$ and $\overrightarrow{FH}$.
(i) Describe the similarities and differences between $\overrightarrow{HE}$ and $\overrightarrow{EH}$.

Using your findings in parts (h) and (i) of question 3, answer the following.

4   If $\overrightarrow{AB} = \begin{pmatrix} 1 \\ 4 \end{pmatrix}$ what is the column vector $\overrightarrow{BA}$?

5   If $\overrightarrow{XY} = \begin{pmatrix} 0 \\ 2 \end{pmatrix}$ what is the column vector $\overrightarrow{YX}$?

6   If $\overrightarrow{PQ} = \begin{pmatrix} -5 \\ 3 \end{pmatrix}$ what is the column vector $\overrightarrow{QP}$?

7   If $\overrightarrow{LM} = \begin{pmatrix} -8 \\ -9 \end{pmatrix}$ what is the column vector $\overrightarrow{ML}$?

8   If $\overrightarrow{RS} = \begin{pmatrix} -10 \\ 0 \end{pmatrix}$ what is the column vector $\overrightarrow{SR}$?

Handling data 1

Cumulative frequency graphs

Measures of spread

Simply looking at the mean of a set of data can be misleading. Look at these job adverts.

Both appear to be offering similar salaries. However, the individual salaries of the five existing employees in each shop are given below.

| Daily Cooperative | €15 000 | €15 000 | €15 000 | €15 000 | €15 000 |
| Daily Bread | | €10 000 | €10 000 | €10 000 | €10 000 | €35 000 |

The one large salary of €35 000 skews the mean employee salary of Daily Bread. Therefore an idea of the **range** of the salaries would also be useful. The range is worked out by simply subtracting the smallest value from the largest value.

Daily Cooperative range is   €15 000 − €15 000 = €0
Daily Bread range is   €35 000 − €10 000 = €25 000

This indicates that within the Daily Bread shop there is a wide range of salaries. In the Daily Cooperative shop, all salaries are the same.

A more sophisticated measure of spread involves the use of **cumulative frequency**. The cumulative frequency is useful for calculating the median of large sets of data, or of grouped or continuous data – something which until now we have not been able to do.

Calculating the cumulative frequency is done by adding up the frequencies as we go along, that is producing a 'running total'.

Worked example

Two farmers pick 60 apples at random from their orchard. Each of the apples is weighed and the results are entered into a grouped frequency table as shown.

Farmer A

Grouped mass (g)	Frequency	Cumulative frequency
$100 < x \leqslant 125$	3	3
$125 < x \leqslant 150$	7	10
$150 < x \leqslant 175$	12	22
$175 < x \leqslant 200$	18	40
$200 < x \leqslant 225$	14	54
$225 < x \leqslant 250$	4	58
$250 < x \leqslant 275$	1	59
$275 < x \leqslant 300$	1	60

Farmer B

Grouped mass (g)	Frequency	Cumulative frequency
$100 < x \leqslant 125$	0	0
$125 < x \leqslant 150$	0	0
$150 < x \leqslant 175$	2	2
$175 < x \leqslant 200$	24	26
$200 < x \leqslant 225$	32	58
$225 < x \leqslant 250$	2	60
$250 < x \leqslant 275$	0	60
$275 < x \leqslant 300$	0	60

(a) Plot a cumulative frequency graph showing the masses of the apples for each farmer.

(b) Calculate the median apple mass for each farmer.

(a)

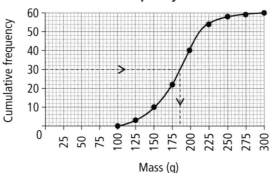

Cumulative frequency for farmer A

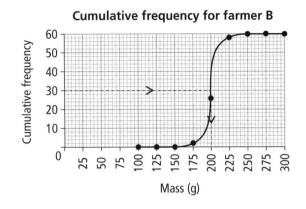

Note that the cumulative frequency data is plotted against the *upper boundary* of each class interval and *not* in the middle.

(b) The median of grouped data can be found from a cumulative frequency graph by reading across from the middle value of the cumulative frequency axis, seeing where it intersects with the curve, and then reading down to the mass axis.

From the graphs it can be seen that the median mass for farmer A ≈ 185 g and the median mass for farmer B ≈ 200 g.

The median results indicate that, on average, farmer B's apples are heavier than those of farmer A.

However, the tables of results show that there is a big difference in the spread of the farmers' apples. This is not apparent just from looking at the median values.

A cumulative frequency graph can also give a good indication of spread if the cumulative frequency axis is seen in terms of **percentiles**.

A percentile scale divides the cumulative frequency axis into hundredths. The maximum value on the cumulative frequency scale is called the **100th percentile**. Other important points on the cumulative frequency scale are:

the **median**, the **50th percentile**
the **lower quartile**, the **25th percentile**
the **upper quartile**, the **75th percentile**

A good measure of spread is to look at the middle 50% of the results and see their range. This range is calculated by subtracting the lower quartile value from the upper quartile value. This range is known as the **inter-quartile range**. Therefore:

inter-quartile range = upper quartile − lower quartile

Worked example

(a) Calculate the inter-quartile range from each of the farmers' cumulative frequency graphs in the previous example.

(b) Comment on the meaning of the inter-quartile range results.

(a)

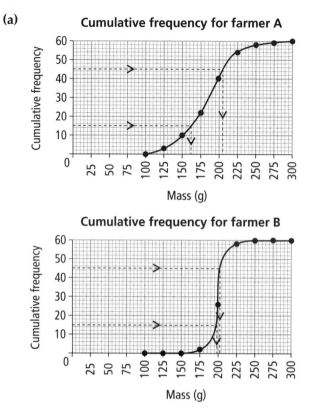

Cumulative frequency for farmer A

Cumulative frequency for farmer B

The results can be summarised in a table:

	Upper quartile	Lower quartile	Inter-quartile range
Farmer A	205	162	$205 - 162 = 43$
Farmer B	202	198	$202 - 198 = 4$

(b) The inter-quartile range results show that, for the middle 50% of results, Farmer A's apples have a greater spread of mass. Farmer B's apples have a more consistent mass as the middle 50% differ by only 4 g.

EXERCISE 24.1

You will need graph paper for this exercise.

1   Two classes A and B take the same mathematics test. Their results are presented in these tables.

Class A

Grouped percentage	Frequency
$0 < x \leqslant 20$	1
$20 < x \leqslant 40$	3
$40 < x \leqslant 60$	16
$60 < x \leqslant 80$	8
$80 < x \leqslant 100$	2

Class B

Grouped percentage	Frequency
$0 < x \leqslant 20$	0
$20 < x \leqslant 40$	0
$40 < x \leqslant 60$	25
$60 < x \leqslant 80$	4
$80 < x \leqslant 100$	1

(a) Construct a cumulative frequency table for each class.
(b) On separate grids, plot a cumulative frequency graph for each class.
(c) From your graphs, deduce the median test score for each class.
(d) Calculate the inter-quartile range for each class.
(e) What do your answers to (c) and (d) tell you about the test results of the two classes?

2 The heights of 50 boys and 50 girls are measured. The data is presented in these two tables.

Boys

Grouped height (cm)	Frequency
$120 < x \leqslant 130$	3
$130 < x \leqslant 140$	5
$140 < x \leqslant 150$	9
$150 < x \leqslant 160$	20
$160 < x \leqslant 170$	12
$170 < x \leqslant 180$	1

Girls

Grouped height (cm)	Frequency
$120 < x \leqslant 130$	6
$130 < x \leqslant 140$	9
$140 < x \leqslant 150$	23
$150 < x \leqslant 160$	8
$160 < x \leqslant 170$	3
$170 < x \leqslant 180$	1

(a) Construct a cumulative frequency table for the boys and one for the girls.
(b) On separate grids, plot a cumulative frequency graph for each.
(c) From your graphs, deduce the median heights of the boys and the girls.
(d) Calculate the inter-quartile range for each.
(e) What do your answers to (c) and (d) tell you about the heights of the boys and girls in this survey?

3 An office worker gets to work by car, using one of two routes. The first route is by motorway; the second avoids the motorway and uses smaller roads. The office worker records the time taken to travel to work by both methods over a number of occasions. The results are presented in these frequency tables.

Motorway

Grouped time (min)	Frequency
$20 < t \leqslant 30$	10
$30 < t \leqslant 40$	3
$40 < t \leqslant 50$	2
$50 < t \leqslant 60$	0
$60 < t \leqslant 70$	3
$70 < t \leqslant 80$	1
$80 < t \leqslant 90$	0
$90 < t \leqslant 100$	1

Smaller roads

Grouped time (min)	Frequency
$30 < t \leqslant 40$	1
$40 < t \leqslant 50$	18
$50 < t \leqslant 60$	1
$60 < t \leqslant 70$	0

(a) Construct a cumulative frequency table for each route.
(b) On separate grids, plot a cumulative frequency graph for each route.
(c) From your graphs, deduce the median time taken to travel by each route.
(d) Calculate the inter-quartile range for each route.
(e) What do your answers to (c) and (d) tell you about the difference in times taken to travel to work?

4   The maximum daily temperatures in two holiday resorts during the month of August are given in the tables.

Resort A

Grouped max. daily temperature (°C)	Frequency
$18 < t \leqslant 20$	6
$20 < t \leqslant 22$	3
$22 < t \leqslant 24$	3
$24 < t \leqslant 26$	5
$26 < t \leqslant 28$	5
$28 < t \leqslant 30$	9

Resort B

Grouped max. daily temperature (°C)	Frequency
$18 < t \leqslant 20$	0
$20 < t \leqslant 22$	0
$22 < t \leqslant 24$	28
$24 < t \leqslant 26$	3
$26 < t \leqslant 28$	0
$28 < t \leqslant 30$	0

(a) Construct a cumulative frequency table for each resort.
(b) On separate grids, plot a cumulative frequency graph for each resort.
(c) From your graphs, deduce the median maximum daily temperature for each resort.
(d) Calculate the inter-quartile range for each resort.
(e) What do your answers to (c) and (d) tell you about the maximum daily temperatures during August at the resorts?

5   1000 pupils sat a mathematics exam. Their percentage scores are shown in this grouped frequency table.

Grouped percentage	Frequency
$0 < x \leqslant 10$	26
$10 < x \leqslant 20$	44
$20 < x \leqslant 30$	56
$30 < x \leqslant 40$	62
$40 < x \leqslant 50$	80
$50 < x \leqslant 60$	126
$60 < x \leqslant 70$	245
$70 < x \leqslant 80$	148
$80 < x \leqslant 90$	131
$90 < x \leqslant 100$	82

(a) Construct a cumulative frequency table of the pupils' results.

(b) Plot a cumulative frequency graph of the results.

(c) The examination board decides that a student should be awarded an A grade if they achieve over 73% in the exam. Estimate, from your graph, the number of students being awarded an A grade.

(d) Students achieving a score in the range 52% to 64% are awarded a C grade. Estimate from your graph the number of students being awarded a C grade.

(e) It is found that the bottom 16% of students failed. Estimate from your graph the percentage score corresponding to the pass mark in the exam.

Investigation

Scientists and environmentalists keep a lot of data on living things to increase their understanding of the world and also to monitor changes that occur.

You will be collecting data on a leaf of your choice.

1   Collect about 30 leaves of the same type – avoid picking them directly from the tree/bush, try to pick them from the ground.

2   Measure the length and width of each leaf – you will need to decide beforehand what you consider to be the length/width of a leaf (for example, does the length include the stalk?).

3   Record your results in a table.

4   Plot graphs to display your data clearly (this could be done using a spreadsheet). Examples include:
    • a scatter graph of length against width
    • a cumulative frequency graph of the leaf lengths.

5   Write a short report on your findings.

ICT activity

This graph shows the graph of $y = x^2$.

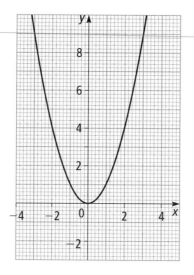

- Using a graph plotter such as Autograph, Omnigraph or a graphical calculator, try to produce these quadratic graphs on the screen.

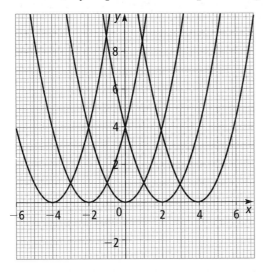

Write each of the quadratic equations in the form $y = (x + a)^2$. What do you notice about the position of the graph and its equation?

- Try to produce the following quadratic graphs on the screen.

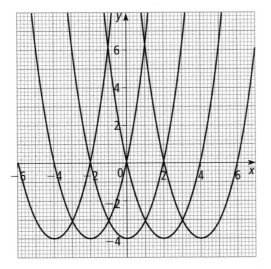

Write each of the quadratic equations in the form $y = (x + a)(x + b)$. What do you notice about the shape of the graph and its equation?

Summary

At the end of this section you should know:
* ★ • how to work with percentage problems in reverse
* ★ • how to plot a graph to represent a quadratic equation
* ★ • how to use the graph of a quadratic equation to find its solution
* ★ • how to form quadratic equations from problems and then solve them graphically
* ★ • how to describe a translation using a column vector
* ★ • how to translate an object by a given column vector
* ★ • how to construct a cumulative frequency table from a frequency table
* ★ • how to plot a cumulative frequency graph
* ★ • how to estimate the median from a cumulative frequency graph
* ★ • how to estimate the upper and lower quartiles from a cumulative frequency graph
* ★ • how to calculate the inter-quartile range
* ★ • the significance of the inter-quartile range as a measure of spread.

Review 6A

1 A house is sold for €250 000. This represents a 15% increase in price since it was last sold. Calculate the previous selling price of the house. Give your answer correct to 3 significant figures.

2 Calculate the value of X in each case.
   (a) 80% of X is 150   (b) 5% of X is 320   (c) 150% of X is 100

3 (a) Plot the quadratic equation $y = x^2 + x - 9$ on a co-ordinate grid for x values in the range $-4 \leqslant x \leqslant 4$.
   (b) Use your graph to solve the equation $x^2 + x - 9 = 0$.

4 (a) Plot the quadratic equation $y = x^2 + 4x + 4$ on a co-ordinate grid for x values in the range $-4 \leqslant x \leqslant 0$.
   (b) Use your graph to solve the equation $x^2 + 4x + 4 = 0$.

5 These two triangles have dimensions as shown. The area of the larger triangle is four times that of the smaller one.

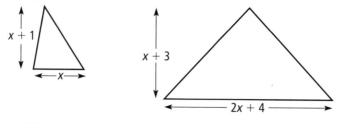

   (a) Write an expression for the area of the smaller triangle.
   (b) Write an expression for the area of the larger triangle.
   (c) Form an equation linking the areas of the two triangles.

(d) Rearrange the equation in the form $ax^2 + bx + c = 0$.

(e) Plot a graph to represent the equation on a grid with x values in the range $-3 \leqslant x \leqslant 6$.

(f) Use your graph to give an approximate solution for the value of x.

6 Write in words the translation represented by each of these vectors.

(a) $\begin{pmatrix} 3 \\ 6 \end{pmatrix}$

(b) $\begin{pmatrix} 4 \\ -2 \end{pmatrix}$

7 Copy this diagram.

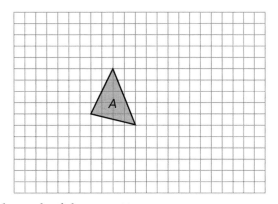

Translate triangle A by each of these vectors.

$$B = \begin{pmatrix} 6 \\ 0 \end{pmatrix} \quad C = \begin{pmatrix} -1 \\ -5 \end{pmatrix} \quad D = \begin{pmatrix} -6 \\ 3 \end{pmatrix}$$

8 A company does a survey to find how long it takes its employees to travel to work in the morning. A sample of 50 employees are chosen at random and their travel times are shown in this table.

Time (mins)	Frequency	Cumulative frequency
0–	2	
10–	5	
20–	8	
30–	4	
40–	14	
50–	15	
60–70	2	

(a) Copy the table and complete the cumulative frequency column.

(b) Plot a cumulative frequency curve of the results.

(c) From your graph, estimate the median travelling time for the employees.

(d) If all 50 employees left home at 8.00 am, estimate from your graph how many would have arrived at work by 8.30 am.

(e) If all 50 employees left home at 8.00 am, at what time would you expect 80% of the employees to be at work?

Review 6B

1 A one-year-old car is sold for €30 000. This represents a 30% depreciation in price. Calculate the original price of the car when new. Give your answer correct to 3 significant figures.

2 Calculate the value of A in each case.
   (a) 55% of A is 130
   (b) 2% of A is 0.2
   (c) 180% of A is 1

3 (a) Plot the quadratic equation $y = 2x^2 - x - 3$ on a grid with x values in the range $-2 \leqslant x \leqslant 2$.
   (b) Use your graph to solve the equation $2x^2 - x = 3$.

4 (a) Plot the quadratic equation $y = x^2 - x + 1$ on a grid with x values in the range $-2 \leqslant x \leqslant 3$.
   (b) Explain, using your graph, why the quadratic $x^2 - x + 1 = 0$ has no solution.

5 Two cuboids A and B have dimensions as shown.

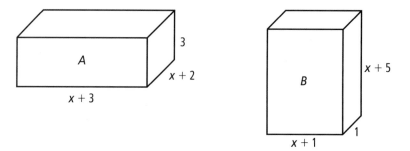

The volume of cuboid A is four times that of cuboid B.
   (a) Write an expression for the volume of cuboid A.
   (b) Write an expression for the volume of cuboid B.
   (c) Form an equation linking the volumes of the two cuboids.
   (d) Rearrange the equation in the form $ax^2 + bx + c = 0$.
   (e) Plot the equation on a grid with x values in the range $-10 \leqslant x \leqslant 2$.
   (f) Use your graph to solve the equation and find values for x.
   (g) Use your answer to (f) to write the dimensions of each cuboid.

6   Write in words the translation represented by each of these vectors.

(a) $\begin{pmatrix} 1 \\ 0 \end{pmatrix}$ (b) $\begin{pmatrix} -3 \\ 5 \end{pmatrix}$

7

Describe the following translations using column vectors.
(a) Translation from A to B
(b) Translation from A to C
(c) Translation from A to D

8   100 pupils sit a mathematics exam. Their percentages are given in the table.

Percentage	Frequency	Cumulative frequency
0–	7	
20–	15	
40–	38	
60–	14	
80–100	26	

(a) Copy the table and complete the cumulative frequency column.
(b) Plot a cumulative frequency curve of the results.
(c) From your graph, estimate the median percentage score.
(d) Calculate the inter-quartile range of the results.
(e) The bottom 30% of the pupils did not pass the exam. What percentage score was the pass mark for this exam?

 Checkpoint questions
Some advice on answering exam
questions is given on page iii.

SECTION SEVEN

Number

1   Write 2 167 000 in standard form.   ....

2   Alec measures the length of a line accurately.
    His answer, correct to 1 decimal place, is 42.7 cm.
    What is the greatest line of the line?   ....

3   Work out the value of $(1.72 \times 10^7) \times (3.46 \times 10^{12})$.   ....

Algebra

1   Solve these simultaneous equations to find the value of x and y.
    $2x + 3y = 24$ $5x - 3y = 18$

    $x =$ ....

    $y =$ ....

2   Find the two possible values of x which satisfy the equation $x^2 - x - 12 = 0$.

    $x =$ ....

    $x =$ ....

3   A water tank is emptied through a hose pipe.
    The volume of water in the tank is measured every minute.
    The graph below shows this information.

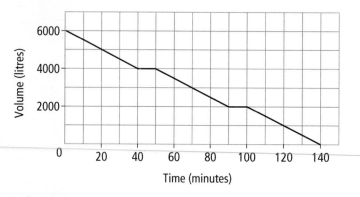

(a) How much water is in the tank at the start?

                                                .... litres

(b) The water is turned off twice.
     How long is the water turned off for altogether?

                                                .... minutes

(c) Work out the rate of flow of water through the hose pipe.
     Do not include the time when the water is turned off.

                                                .... litres/minute

(d) Another tank contains 8100 litres of water. It is emptied at a rate of 30 litres/minute. How long will it take to empty this tank?

.... minutes

[23 October–10 November 2000, 1112/2, question 5]

Shape, space and measures

1

Scale: 1 cm represents 10 km

The diagram, which **is drawn accurately**, shows part of the journey of a yacht.
The yacht leaves P and sails 100 km in a straight line to buoy A.
The yacht then sails 80 km due south to another buoy B.
It then turns and sails straight back to P.

(a) Measure and write down the **bearing** of A from P.

.... °

(b) Complete the diagram to show the remainder of the journey.
Show clearly the position of buoy B.

(c) (i) Measure the distance on your drawing from buoy B to P.

.... cm

(ii) What is the real distance from buoy B to P?

.... km

[23 October–10 November 2000, 1112/2, question 3]

2   A builder uses a wooden framework to support a semi-circular brick arch while it is being built. The diagram shows this.

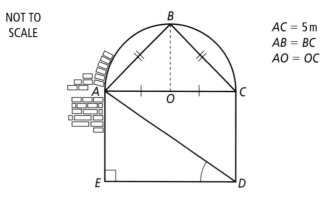

NOT TO
SCALE

$AC = 5\,m$
$AB = BC$
$AO = OC$

(a) Calculate the length of AB.

$AB =$ .... m

(b) $AE = CD = 3\,m$
Calculate angle ADE.
Give your answer correct to the nearest whole degree.

$ADE =$ .... $^\circ$

[23 October–10 November 2000, 1112/2, question 9]